DATE DUE

Hans G. Jellen
John R. Verduin, Jr.

Handbook *for* Differential Education *of the* Gifted

A Taxonomy
of 32 Key Concepts

Southern Illinois University Press
Carbondale and Edwardsville

Edited by Yvonne D. Mattson
Designed by Kathleen Giencke

89 88 87 86   4 3 2 1

Library of Congress Cataloging-in-Publication Data

Jellen, Hans G.
  Handbook for differential education of the gifted

  Bibliography: p.
    1. Gifted children—Education—United States—
Curricula.   2. Curriculum enrichment—United
States.   3. Curriculum planning—United States.   4. High
schools—United States—Elective system.   I. Verduin, John R.
II. Title.   III. Title: Differential education of the gifted.
LC3993.9.J44   1986   371.95′3   85-27703
ISBN 0-8093-1278-6

To all gifted learners, who deserve
the chance to utilize their full
potential in all fields of knowledge

To the memory of
Herbert Jellen,
John R. Verduin, Sr.,
and Dorothy E. Verduin

CONTENTS

Appendixes

Bibliography

FOREWORD

This study of the conceptual foundations of education for persons at the extremes of human potential for thought and action constitutes for both the serious student and the accomplished scholar an unusually useful *Handbook for Differential Education of the Gifted*.

Essentially two main bodies of thought have been developed by the authors: the first an explicit and well-reasoned foundation in the form of a taxonomy for special education of gifted youth and the second an economical set of relevant concepts (n = 32) central to the theory and practice of differential education of the gifted (DEG). As a scientific work, Jellen and Verduin's *Handbook* constitutes in a true sense a conceptualized plan for the field of DEG that, so far, has been nonexistent. The book offers, for this conceptually impoverished and insufficiently developed area of knowledge and for students and scholars who demand deeper inquiry, the following significant attributes:

(a) *An integrated conceptualization of DEG* appropriate for the potentials of gifted persons, studiously derived from and constructed out of the more fundamental philosophical and educational thought currently available in international reference texts.

(b) *A conceptual economy for DEG* based on a taxonomy of 32 generic concepts and terms that subsumes the indeterminable amount of superficial nomenclature that dominates the current DEG scene.

(c) *A concise, explanatory, and well-researched interpretation for each DEG concept* in order to facilitate applications to the realities of research, training programs, and instructional content as well as educational methodology.

There is at the present time among the leaders in DEG some hope and expectancy that conditions as they emerge and unfold toward the later years of the present century will support a turn toward the more solid intellectual foundations that are the necessary precursors of more authentic professional practice based on sound theory. This DEG handbook is a contribution— and indeed a considerable one—toward these desirable and overdue ends.

VIRGIL S. WARD

PREFACE

Public school education in general seems to be fermenting at this time as educators and lay people alike review criticisms evolving from the numerous "national" reports and studies. At the same time we are being inundated with current and projected advancements in science, technology, and communication and information systems. Finally, social and economic concerns exist, demographic shifts occur, globalization or "earth as one" is discussed, and numerous other problems and issues confront us.

One facet of the total educational enterprise, the education of our gifted young people, should be a significant part of the total reevaluation and development process. We simply must do more for our gifted learners. Progress in designing meaningful empirical research in a given field depends largely on the existence of a precise classification of relevant terminology. A defensible classification of this sort is also the necessary prerequisite for the advancement of research in DEG. No such conceptualization of DEG exists in today's literature. Therefore, little meaningful research in the areas of theory and practice has been produced during the last twenty years since Ward's original inception of a curricular foundation for DEG. We must bring greater theory, structure, and organization to the education of the gifted. This *Handbook* attempts to move the field of differential education for the gifted (DEG) from a loose, atheoretical base to a more precise, theoretical position for advancing this important phase of education. In addition, we must provide better and more precise learning experiences for our gifted so that they can provide leadership as knowledge producers in helping to solve the above-mentioned problems as well as taking leadership roles in the arts, humanities, and other important areas.

This *Handbook* presents an economized and conceptualized taxonomy of important concepts for DEG. Its basic purpose is to foster the clarification and advancement of theory and practice in DEG. It is designed for educators interested in this field, but it can also be most useful to other educational practitioners and to those who conduct honors programs at various colleges and universities.

Part 1 introduces the *Handbook* by describing the key features. It discusses the development of the taxonomy, the four major, relevant factors in it, and the 32 DEG concepts. It further discusses the four justifications for the taxonomy in a procedural democracy. Finally, it discusses briefly the application of the taxonomy for the advancement of DEG theory and practice through empirical research and pedagogical applications. Part 2 offers the theoretical treatment of the 32 DEG concepts within the framework of the taxonomy. This is done by breaking down the four major factors of the taxonomy and then offering the descriptive and prescriptive treatments and discussions of each DEG concept.

Included also within this *Handbook* is an extensive bibliography that should prove most useful to the researcher and practitioner of DEG. Furthermore, four appendixes are included, which can aid the practitioner in culture-fair identification procedures and in unit construction and program evaluation. The reader should find these very useful tools for implementation and for the entire process of DEG. It should be noted that Appendix A could be most meaningful to researchers who wish to record vital data on gifted learners' behavior in longitudinal studies, which, in turn, could advance DEG on empirical grounds.

The ordered listings of DEG concepts, the DEG taxonomy, and the efforts to prescribe methods as well as content and to screen relevant bibliographical references from international sources should lead to a uniformly higher plan of educational practice in DEG here and abroad. Of course, the taxonomized concepts and terms used in this DEG handbook are human inventions, like all scientific concepts. They are abstractions whose existence or nonexistence cannot be proven. Ordered and defined concepts can, however, be useful or useless; they cannot be true or false. It is only by this criterion that the 32 concepts discussed here should be judged.

In any case, the initial intent of the authors remains the same, namely to bring consistency, order, cohesiveness, and conceptual meaning to a field that can presently be described as rather loose, divergent, inconsistent, and atheoretical.

ACKNOWLEDGMENTS

We want to take this opportunity to acknowledge all those individuals who have continuously encouraged us to complete this complex but long-overdue endeavor.

Professor Virgil Ward and Professor Peter Hackett (University of Virginia) as well as Professor Brian Holmes and Professor T. W. Moore (University of London) laid the theoretical foundations of this conceptual handbook for differential education for the gifted (DEG). Their insights in educational theory, comparative taxonomization, and conceptual analysis made it possible for us to formulate and to defend this economical set of relevant DEG concepts.

Several doctoral students at the University of London Institute of Education provided us with multilingual nuances and diverse cultural meanings of the thirty-two concepts addressed in this DEG handbook. In addition to such clarifications of terminology, they also provided us with additional research on the selected concepts.

Linda O'Brien assisted us with the formulation of a personalysis for DEG. She also worked in close collaboration with Professor David Goh of Guidance and Educational Psychology and Professors Rudy Lorber, Ron Schmuck and Tom Shill of Psychology at Southern Illinois University in Carbondale.

Robert L. Richardson and Don G. Smith worked with us on the research and writing that applied to the six content areas of Phenix's curricular foundations (1964) adapted for DEG and the four sociological concepts relevant to DEG in the context of Jellen's taxonomy (1984).

ACKNOWLEDGMENTS

Our gratitude must be expressed to Mary Jane Schaaf, especially, and to Charlene Oliver, Dawn Buff, Ginger Watson, Jennifer Cloos, and Steven Wisecarver for their outstanding work in typing and retyping this manuscript in its preparation.

Finally, to our families, Mrs. Ilse Jellen, residing in the Federal Republic of Germany, and Janet, John, and Susan Verduin, we express our appreciation for their continued support in this endeavor.

Part One

INTRODUCTION

DESCRIPTION OF KEY FEATURES

Purpose and Scope of the DEG Handbook

Educational glossaries of a general kind do not preclude the usefulness of this handbook for differential education of the gifted (DEG). In the framework of a research study, this document offers in its second part DEG categories and DEG abstractions that should move thinking and action toward a DEG theory on the whole for stated groups (that is, educators interested in DEG) and stated purposes (that is, clarification and advancement of theory and practice in DEG).

The ordered listing of 32 terms, the taxonomical presentation, and the descriptions, prescriptions, and follow-up discussions of these DEG concepts are intended to provide educational researchers, planners, and practitioners with an instrument of reasoned explanation and consistent thinking for the formulation of educational policies that will affect the education of gifted learners.

The Master List of DEG Concepts

The precision and exactitude of this DEG theory rests upon the accuracy of 32 generic terms intended as a theoretical foundation for DEG. Further additions and revisions are, of course, expected as the field advances its research efforts. The validity of the 32 concepts was corroborated by conducting comparative research in international references and DEG texts. So-called expert judgment was set aside as unacceptable verification of the master list, since many DEG contemporaries exhibit severe theoretical gaps in their conceptualizations of the field. The master list, then, attempts to break the ethnocentricity and collective subjectivity that permeate the contemporary theory and practice of DEG.

TAXONOMY FOR DEG

Jellen and White (1980) made the first attempt to classify concepts associated with DEG. Both designed seven clusters for fifty concepts in the form of a summative matrix. The matrix itself is a good representation of DEG terminology found in the literature and thought of the American DEG scene today. What is lacking, however, is a hierarchical ordering of these clusters and an identification of meaningful concepts that predominantly should be the province of DEG specialists. In addition to these shortcomings, many educators have failed to provide a set of theoretical positions necessary to justify their clusters of DEG concepts. Jellen (1981) finally added theoretical considerations to a new list of 32 key concepts that can be defended within the context of DEG.

These 32 concepts have been linked with four factors or variables to be addressed in the design of curricular theory (Holmes, 1981). Each factor is backed by theoretical positions and recommended practices for DEG. The outcome is a taxonomy for DEG (see Table 5, p. 000) which ranks and organizes objectives for DEG into meaningful categories and logically defensible concepts. Such a classification system adds order, clarity, significance, and conceptual meaning to the atheoretical nature of so-called "gifted, talented" or "creative" education.

The Developmental Stages of the DEG Taxonomy

The taxonomy was developed in four stages, all of which are essential to the conceptualization and meaning of DEG.

Stage One. The first stage involved the identification of "relevant factors" necessary for the formulation of a curricular theory as it applies to DEG. The factors divide and rank DEG into four major areas of concern: the nature of the gifted learner, the role of the DEG educationist, the demands of knowledge, and the needs of society. These four factors or variables represent accepted theoretical assumptions about curricular theory held by leading educationists such as Peters (1966), Bernstein (1973), Moore (1974), Ward (1980) and Holmes (1981). The resulting outcome is a fourfold taxonomization for DEG.

Stage Two. "Theoretical positions" were formulated for

each of the four preceding factors. These positions are consistent with education research in concept theory (Moore, 1974), psychometrics (Eysenck, 1979), pedagogy (Peters, 1966), epistemology (Phenix, 1964), and sociology (Bernstein, 1973). An integral aspect of this phase was the development of a theoretical rationale to guide the conceptualization and organization of the remaining divisions within each categorization.

Stage Three. The theoretical positions for each of the four taxonomical clusters made it possible for a conceptual frame of 32 "subsequent key concepts" to emerge. Again, each concept is backed by careful research in the psychological, pedagogical, epistemological, and sociological foundations of education and their specific applications to DEG.

Stage Four. "Recommended practices" constitute a logical conclusion for each of the preceding categories. The completed taxonomy was then checked for consistency. A final examination was made on the reliability of the classes in the taxonomy by comparing it to Ward's axioms (1980). All criteria for classification were essentially in agreement with Ward's earlier propositions.

The Meaning of the Four Factors within the DEG Taxonomy

Within the framework of the four relevant factors or variables adopted from Holmes (1981), the taxonomy's major features can be highlighted by the following division (cf. Jellen's Taxonomy for DEG, Table 5, p. 000).

Factor One: The Nature of the Gifted Learner. The nature of giftedness is defined as a mental construct rather than a single concept. Cognitive, affective, *and* conative abilities contribute to the multifaceted nature of the gifted mind on the whole. Cognitive operations bring awareness to complex and abstract information processes; affective operations are emotional sequences which vary in intensity, similarity, and polarity; and conative operations, which are frequently ignored by educators, supply the motive power to all activities that are the means to the attainment of desired ends.

Every one of these mental domains of a gifted mind must be addressed and assessed for meaningful identification to take place. Subsequently, early and valid selection procedures must follow a multifaceted assessment technique of the mental construct of giftedness composed of six key concepts that reflect cognitive, affective, and conative capabilities. The corresponding identification procedures must be supported by valid and reliable psychometric instruments. Nominational devices are the least recommended and most subjective screening devices for identification purposes.

Factor Two: The Role of the DEG Educationist. DEG educationists must be carefully selected and trained to fulfill the complex tasks affiliated with the teaching, facilitation (with outside mentors), and counseling of gifted learners. These roles will ensure academic, personal, *and* social development of the entire gifted learner. A miseducation of the gifted occurs when early vocational training or acceleration in idiosyncratic particulars replaces a general but differentiated curriculum which must satisfy the canons of intellectual challenge, socio-emotional stability and moral responsibility (Jellen, 1984). These important educational objectives for the DEG educationist have become secondary in the United States and abroad; utilitarian exploitation of gifted youths seems to be the rule rather than the exception (Jellen, 1985a; Ward, 1961). Therefore, DEG educationists must transcend the traditional role of classroom teachers or aptitudinal trainers by utilizing educational opportunities in and out of school that should contribute to the holistic development of the gifted individual. Mentorships, internships and/or tutorials with other gifted individuals such as local innovators, inventors, writers, reformers, and/or composers who have the potential to instill early vision and mission in these potential knowledge producers. Knowledge producers are those who produce and evaluate new knowledge from existing knowledge and therefore differ from the traditional "knowledge utilizers." Three out of the seven key concepts under this factor remind the DEG educationist to build leaders with a character capable of socially responsible and responsive knowledge production in all fields of knowledge. Knowledge production is seen as a sign and proof of giftedness since it transcends such notions as the factual knowledge regurgitation and utilization so apparent in most regular school settings.

Factor Three: The Demands of Knowledge. This factor is a radical departure from the factual knowledge consumption and regurgitation that dominate in the lock-step-fashion, "normal schooling" in the Western world. Qualitative differentiation and articulation of contents, methods, and evaluations are demands for generativity or a quest of the unknown. Hypothetical thinking, great ideas, and generic concepts in ethics (moral knowledge and know-how), synnoetics (personal/social knowledge and know-how), and synoptics (philosophic-historical knowledge and know-how) embrace generativity and compose a meaningful curricular DEG core as a means to nurture high degrees of general intellectual ability in all gifted students. The expected outcome is a mental restructuring of values, attitudes, and beliefs toward more altruistic, cooperative, and responsive-responsible behaviors.

Empirics (scientific knowledge and know-how), esthetics (artistic knowledge and know-how), and symbolics (communicative knowledge and know-how) contain a wealth of curricular electives for the nurturing of specific aptitudes or talents displayed by most gifted students. Here, too, emphasis should be placed on learning how to learn, to question, to apply, to explore, and to produce new ideas, concepts, and hypotheses.

The six pedagogical methods or approaches recommended have the potential to reinforce problem solving, to pursue a wide range of interests, to discover new ways of doing things, to make connections between structures and functions in all types of knowledge, and to enjoy learning through student-designed simulations or projects. These approaches have the greatest potential to elicit *knowledge production*—the sign and proof of giftedness.

Achievement, evaluation, and observation are the last three concepts considered under this factor and should be rigorously applied not only to the gifted learner but also to the DEG educationist and program. The DEG setting in a given community must become a place of experimentation, exploration, and innovation. Achievement through DEG implies progress in academic, personal, and social terms, benefiting not only the gifted individual but also the educationist, the sponsoring community, and society at large.

Factor Four: The Needs of Society. All societies are in need of socially responsive-responsible knowledge production. This is particularly true in a rapidly changing world confronted with a knowledge and population explosion, as well as an explosion of public expectations. DEG becomes, therefore, a means to explore, to evaluate, to adopt, and to adapt to change. This pragmatic-revisionist role of DEG counteracts the elitist stratification and social isolation of gifted youth. This last tenet in the taxonomy exposes the gifted to programmatic and differentiated enrichment on a part-time basis, supplementing but not supplanting regular schooling. This form of programmatic enrichment will give these brilliant young minds an opportunity to meet, to interact, and to learn about contents not covered in normal schools. Rotation of the gifted will also guarantee that a maximum number of students get a chance to participate in DEG. Learning how to learn, to adapt, to be productive, and to grow must be the essence of DEG in a free, democratic, and advanced society. DEG must, therefore, reflect liberal, democratic, and progressive values in academic, personal, and social terms.

Descriptive Treatment of the 32 DEG Concepts

These introductory definitions provide a brief and non-controversial description of the field's terminology as it is increasingly understood and accepted in the Western world interested in DEG.

The writers of this handbook made a deliberate attempt to relate the generic meanings of these terms, derived from international and reputable reference texts for education and psychology, directly to DEG. The outcome is a "Dictionary for DEG."

Prescriptive Treatment of the 32 DEG Concepts

Whereas the descriptive treatment offers generic definitions of relevant DEG terminology, the prescriptive part is intended to direct and guide both practitioners in classroom operations and theorists in their investigations; this section is specifically designed to advance DEG in theory and practice.

We have reached a consensus on what DEG should be in the context of a procedural democracy by providing the reader with a set of prescriptors that can be defended in light of psychometric, pedagogical, curricular, and sociological theory.

Narrative Treatment of the 32 DEG Concepts

The short and direct follow-up discussions on each of the 32 concepts incorporated a wide range of research findings and illustrative materials formulated by reputable scholars in such areas as psycho-metrics, pedagogy, psychology, epistemology, sociology, education and philosophy.

JUSTIFICATIONS OF THE KEY FEATURES

Together, these 32 topical essays attempt to reveal not only the nature of DEG but also the fourfold justifications for DEG in a procedural democracy (Jellen, 1985b).

Psychological Justifications for DEG in a Procedural Democracy

In spite of the intellectual superiority and enormous potential of gifted students, many of these brilliant individuals display quite early an educational portrait of a different sort. By attending regular schools, they often become educationally retarded through the processes of academic mediocrity and social maladjustment. Newland (1976) states the fact that "many of them tend to perform noticeably below their individual capabilities, with an attendant failure of self-fulfillment and ultimate social loss. . . . [This] calls for preventive efforts on the part of the schools and an understanding of the importance of this condition by parents." (p. 111)

Hollingworth's research (1936) went one step further by warning educators and others of the psychological implications of giftedness that turned gifted learners "sour" and, therefore, made them act "sour giftedly." Her findings are as relevant today as they were in the thirties.

> Academic, personal, and social maladjustments . . . may lead to complete alienation from (the gifted child's) contemporaries in childhood, and to misanthropy in adolescence and adulthood. Particularly deplorable are the struggles of these children against dull or otherwise unworthy adults in authority. The very gifted child or adolescent, perceiving the illogical conduct of those in charge of his affairs, may turn rebellious against all authority and fall into a condi-

tion of negative suggestability—a most unfortunate trend of personality, since the person is then unable to take a co-operative attitude toward authority. (Pp. 277–78)

Cooperation is an essential and civic function in a procedural democracy. The psychological justifications for DEG in a procedural democracy must, therefore, rest on the premise that DEG becomes instrumental to the sound psychological development of gifted young people by providing meaningful academic and developmental experiences that will allow these children to function well in and out of school.

Pedagogical Justifications for DEG in a Procedural Democracy

DEG should provide *gifted teachers* with an opportunity to explore new contents, methods, and evaluations not suited for the regular school populace. This is an additional task of the DEG educationist recruiting those gifted educators who can involve gifted students in contents and activities that have *no* initial appeal to them. This justification intends to counteract the highly student-accommodating nature of so many enrichment programs that exist throughout the United States and that claim to serve the academic and developmental needs of the gifted child (Jellen, 1985a).

The pedagogical justifications for DEG in a procedural democracy rest on the assertion that gifted teachers can be found in regular schools, teachers with a definite need to find an opportunity to interact, to work, and to learn with intellectual peers in an achievement-oriented climate of cooperation and mutual trust. Differential pedagogy serves, then, as a means to challenge or to motivate intellect, to elicit empathy, and to reinforce civic responsibility in all parties involved. These educational objectives for teachers and those who are taught are seen as fundamental to the survival of the democratic process in democratic schools.

Epistemological Justifications for DEG in a Procedural Democracy

DEG is a demand for knowledge production (KP) in the various branches of epistemology. Knowledge production is to be shared with others. These demands for shared knowledge production through DEG require a weak classification and framing of educational knowledge.

Classification of educational knowledge refers not to what is classified but to the relationships between epistemological contents. Thus, classification refers to the degree of insulation and differentiation between curricular contents (Bernstein, 1973, p. 366). The two leading curricular theories in Western Europe, that is encyclopedism (continental Europe) and essentialism (Great Britain), favor strong classification of curricular contents by reinforcing boundary strength as the critical distinguishing feature for a later division of labor (Bernstein, 1973). Strong classification of knowledge codifies and stratifies school curricula according to "academic" or "vocational" contents. Educators in the European gymnasia, lycees and "public" schools learn early that their knowledge is "academic" or "pure" and, therefore, the private and traditional property of a few. This academic or pure knowledge is *not* to be shared with the rest of the populace; thus, academic knowledge tends to be transmitted only to elite pupils who are acceptable to the well-insulated academic communities within these elitist schools. Strong insulation of an exclusively academic curriculum creates a prevailing sense of conformity on matters of class identity and social membership. Both are necessary for the reproduction of class, caste, or social elites (Bernstein, 1973)—antithetical notions in a procedural democracy.

Framing of educational knowledge refers to the degree of control teachers and students possess over the selection, organization, and pacing of contents transmitted and received in the pedagogical relationship (Bernstein, 1973, p. 366). Strong framing reduces the power of the student over what, when, and how he or she perceives predetermined types of knowledge. It also increases the teacher's power and control in the relationship between teachers and students. Evaluation of student progress focuses on excessive testing, which reflects "factual regurgitation of subject matter" (Bernstein, 1973, p. 367). Again, European academic schools favor and reinforce a strong framing of the pedagogical relationship.

Weak classification and framing of educational knowledge justify DEG on epistemological grounds in the context of a procedural democracy. Both principles encourage curricular and pedagogical flexibility, a variety of curricular offerings, and access to *all* forms of knowledge. Weak classification and framing of contents also foster openness in four areas: open communication among faculty members, among students, between students and teachers, as well as within the community at large. Learning how to learn together and produce desired forms of knowledge collectively in all fields of knowledge becomes the focus of interest in designing meaningful curricula for DEG. Such emphasis on ways of knowing, rather than upon factual states of knowledge, is likely to affect not only the pedagogy but also the underlying theory of learning and evaluating in DEG. Learning and evaluating in DEG become more self- or group-regulated, affecting not only the students but also the educationists and the community they serve. The acquisition, production, dissemination, and evaluation of generative knowledge are seen as cooperative and egalitarian efforts (Bernstein, 1973, p. 386).

. The training of leaders in responsible knowledge production within all types of knowledge becomes the attestor of the problem solving that must go on in and out of school. Weak classification and framing of educational knowledge for DEG are seen as preventive measures to be taken in order to avoid elitist stratification, utilitarian exploitation, and social isolation of the gifted.

Sociological Justifications for DEG in a Procedural Democracy

For a procedural democracy to exist and to function, some kind of procedure for consulting citizens must exist so that they can approve or resist authoritative policy and action (Peters, 1966, p. 295). Such procedures always operate within a weak classification and framing of democratic principles. The American Constitution is a perfect example of a procedural democracy since it represents an elaborate attempt to provide citizens with an effective system of checks and balances necessary to safeguard the rights of individuals and minorities. This framework of checks and balances spells out, in the form of amendments, the fundamental principles of fairness, liberty, equality, and respect for others. In order to settle differences, a procedural democracy encourages matters of conflict to be resolved by recourse to reasonable discussion rather than by recourse to force, arbitrary authority, ideology, or belief (Peters, 1966, p. 299).

DEG reinforces procedural democracy by making its educational and developmental offerings available to all students who qualify, regardless of race, color, religion, sex, or creed. DEG must demand from its staff, students, and supporters a commitment to liberty and fairness, as well as a consideration of interests stated by the majority *and* the minorities of a given community. Democratization of DEG provides, therefore, a structured educational situation within a community in which its citizens find democratic procedures operating in an exemplary fashion. There should be some rotation of office, a system of accountability, a sector for public relations, an information center on procedural know-how, and a gifted teaching staff drawn from the entire community. The value of such an exemplary system of democratic functioning within a school system and within a given community lies in its potential as a model and training ground for developing a rational attitude toward authority and subordinates, free information flow and democratic procedures. Thus, DEG becomes the training ground for democratic leadership and academic excellence.

There can be nothing objectionable or elitist about a reasonable, competent student leader with a sense of civic responsibility and a desire to work for or with others on some common task or problem. Student leadership through DEG should only be evaluated or judged for the conscious intentions, competence, and decency with which it discharges its duties in and out of school. The locus of education for democratic leadership asserts that DEG develops a rational, humanistic, and moral attitudes toward the exercising of authority and knowledge production. Leaders of this sort do not simply appear—they have to be trained in ethics and democratic process. DEG has the potential to produce such extraordinary leaders based on the knowledge about the gifted mind, which can operate on high degrees of rational, humanistic, and moral thought (Newland, 1976). There is a desperate need for this kind of leadership. On this sociological premise alone, the writers of this DEG handbook find a sound justification for DEG in the specific contexts of egalitarianism, pragmatism, and procedural democracy.

ADDITIONAL FEATURES

See Also

"See Also" refers the reader to additional DEG concepts that fall under those taxonomical categorizations that help expand the understanding and the implications of the DEG concept under discussion. This feature establishes meaningful connections between the four relevant factors within the taxonomy.

Related Concepts

"Related Concepts" attempts to elucidate the range of different terminologies that can be associated with each DEG concept. This set of terminology is broader and provides additional variance on meanings that might aid DEG research efforts.

Suggested Readings

"Suggested Readings" acknowledges the writings of those scholars and researchers who have achieved distinction through contributions of topical research that falls within the field of DEG. These bibliographical entries also constitute the documentation for the follow-up discussion on each DEG concept.

Appendixes

The appendix section in this handbook provides a detailed overview of the particular essentials concerning "Characterology and Personalysis for DEG" (Appendix A); "Program Evaluation for DEG" (Appendix B); "Unit Construction for DEG" (Appendix C); and "Mental Testing in DEG" (Appendix D). All four appendixes derived logically from the guidelines and procedures that are addressed in the narrative discussions on each concept. This section should be of particular interest to those researchers and practitioners who are concerned with the theoretical and practical advances to be made in DEG. Each appendix can also be linked with the fourfold taxonomization of the field, its subcategories, and the extensive treatment of each concept in the handbook.

Bibliography for DEG

In order to stress the international aspect of the handbook, the authors attempted to present a broad selection of relevant literature. Most entries listed in the handbook were in print at the time this manuscript was prepared.

APPLICATION

Most concepts and related issues addressed in this handbook suggest further considerations and investigations concerning the improvement of this instrument on theoretical and practical grounds.

Considerations for an Advancement of DEG Theory

In order to expand, refine, and/or further economize the handbook's terminology, the following theoretical considerations must be addressed:

1. The 32 concepts in the handbook have been assessed as relevant for inclusion through taxonomical ordering. Any additions must be assessed similarly.
2. Each addition must meaningfully contribute to the four factors within the taxonomy of the field.
3. New inclusions must show the potential for direct application to DEG.
4. New terminology must also find more frequent use in DEG than in other areas of education.
5. If DEG concepts are more frequently used in related fields, then a different meaning for DEG must emerge.
6. Elimination of outdated terminology should not disturb the overall conceptualization of the field, that is, the taxonomization for DEG.
7. New sub-divisions in the taxonomies must correspond to the four factors of educational theory relevant to DEG, that is, the nature of the gifted learner, the role of the DEG educationist, the demands of knowledge, and the needs of society.

Considerations for an Advancement of DEG Practice

Practice, here, refers to empirical research and pedagogical applications.

INTRODUCTION

A. Empirical Research

The main objective here is to have the instrument serve as a catalyst to advance the empirical nature of the field on an international scale. The theoretical framework for DEG, as manifested in the taxonomy, allows for meaningful research to emerge.

Factor One (the nature of the gifted learner) encourages us to see the gifted mind on the whole by broadening the construct of giftedness in addressing the affective and conative components of mental ability as well. There is no need, however, to invent new nomenclature. Instead, one should return to and focus on mental operations that find empirical backing in psychology and psycho-metrics.

Factor Two (the role of the DEG educationist) urges us to approach DEG as an emerging science. Such key terms as "characterology," "differentiation," and "mental testing" serve as constant reminders to advance the field on empirical grounds and to consider the threefold nature of the task of the DEG educationist: the teaching, facilitating, and counseling of the whole gifted person.

Factor Three (the demands of knowledge) requires three generative message systems for DEG: (1) an articulated and a qualitatively differentiated curriculum in all content areas; (2) a relevant methodology; and (3) normative and summative assessment techniques. All three message systems should attempt to shift our educative efforts from mere knowledge consumption and utilization to knowledge production through DEG.

Factor Four (the needs of society) forces leadership into a democratic mold. The outcome of DEG must be democratic leadership and responsive-responsible knowledge production operating on ethical principles and democratic procedures for the sake of personal, social, and academic reform.

These four theoretical propositions determine the application of the handbook as a reference tool for DEG policy. The main use of the instrument will probably be as a reference and revision tool, that is, as a means by which theoreticians and practitioners can make quick reference to those concepts and categories that will assist them in their efforts to overcome the utilitarian shallowness that prevails in much of contemporary DEG research and practice.

B. Pedagogical Applications

The aim of uniting the fragments of DEG with a single work of reference is helpful not only to DEG educationists but to other educators as well. The teacher working in the classroom, the supervisor visiting schools, and the administrator meeting deadlines all reflect involvement in daily school routines. Together, they are kept too busy to be familiar with other subfields of education. Too few of them have time for or access to the latest research and new developments in a given sub-division of education. For this reason, this DEG handbook will become a convenient reference for those not familiar with DEG and its related terminology.

For DEG educationists and practitioners, the pragmatic purpose of the handbook as a piece of reference is self-evident. The most practical and immediate aim of this work is, however, to be of service and guidance to the researchers and practitioners in the field. The entire handbook contains a systematic treatise on each of the four theoretical key factors. With such comprehensive divisions, the work hopes to eventually constitute an authoritative and cohesive reference for DEG psychology, pedagogy, epistemology, and sociology. Out of such theoretical organization of materials and references, so heterogenous and diverse in character, some greater appreciation for DEG theory may evolve and a greater cohesiveness may result in DEG practice as well as research.

REFERENCES

Bernstein, B. 1973. On the classification and framing of educational knowledge. In *Knowledge, education, and cultural change*, ed. R. Brown. London: Tavistock.

Eysenck, H. 1979. *The structure and measurement of intelligence.* New York: Springer.

Hollingworth, L. 1936. The development of personality of highly intelligent children. In *Fifteenth yearbook of the department of elementary school principals*, 274–78. Washington: National Education Association.

Holmes, B. 1981. *Comparative education: Some considerations of method.* London: Allen/Unwin.

Jellen, H., and B. White. 1980. Current thought: 50 contemporary concepts in DEG. In *Differential education for the gifted*, by V. Ward, xxix–lxxi. Los Angeles: National/State Leadership Training Institute on the Gifted and the Talented.

Jellen, H. 1981. *A multi-lingual glossary for differential education for the gifted (DEG)*. Ph.D. diss., University of Virginia.

———. 1985a. Renzulli's enrichment scheme for the gifted: Educational accommodation of the gifted in the American context. *Gifted Education International* 3 (1): 12–17.

———. 1985b. The meaning of and justifications for DEG in a democracy: A taxonomical approach. *Gifted Education International* 3 (2): 94–99.

Moore, T. 1974. *Educational theory: An introduction*. London: Routledge/Kegan.

Newland, T. E. 1976. *The gifted in socio-educational perspective*. Englewood Cliffs, NJ: Prentice/Hall.

Peters, R. S. 1966. *Ethics and education*. London: Allen/Unwin.

Phenix, P. 1964. *Realms of meaning*. New York: McGraw-Hill.

Ward, V. 1961. *Educating the gifted: An axiomatic approach*. Columbus, OH: Merrill.

———. 1980. *Differential education for the gifted*. Los Angeles: National/State Leadership Training Institute on the Gifted and the Talented.

Part Two

TREATMENT OF THE
32 CONCEPTS

TAXONOMIC BREAKDOWN OF THE FOUR MAJOR FACTORS

The second part of this handbook presents (1) an overview of the 32 concepts as they are found within the four major factors of the taxonomy; (2) a taxonomic breakdown and discussion of the 32 concepts according to the four major factors (Tables 1, 2, 3, 4); (3) a taxonomic system of relevant factors, theoretical positions, subsequent key concepts, and recommended practices (Table 5); and (4) the descriptive as well as prescriptive treatment and discussion of each DEG concept within the framework of the four taxonomical factors. The purpose of this section is to impart to the reader a greater understanding of the dimensions of the entire taxonomy.

AN OVERALL LISTING OF THE 32 DEG CONCEPTS

II. The Role of the DEG Educationist

III. The Demands of Knowledge

IV. The Needs of Society

Synthesis: An Emerging DEG Taxonomy

Factor One: The Nature of the Gifted Learner. The nature of giftedness is defined as a mental construct consisting of six key concepts that address cognition, affect, and conation. Cognitive, affective, *and* conative abilities contribute to the multifaceted nature of the gifted mind on the whole.

Factor Two: The Role of the DEG Educationist. DEG educationists are professionals selected and trained to fulfill the complex tasks affiliated with the teaching, facilitation, and counseling of gifted learners. Seven key concepts will insure academic, personal, *and* social development of the entire gifted individual.

Factor Three: The Demands of Knowledge. Qualitative differentiation and articulation of contents, methods, and evaluations are the demands for generativity, knowledge production, or a quest of the unknown. Fifteen key concepts contribute to a meaningful didactic core that will hopefully elevate DEG to a higher plane of educational practice.

Factor Four: The Needs of Society. Four key concepts prevent DEG from becoming a highly elitist, isolated or insulated educational approach. Since all societies are in need of responsive-responsible knowledge production, DEG becomes an educational means to explore, to evaluate, to adopt, and to adapt to change. This pragmatic-revisionist role of DEG counteracts the exclusive subject-specific training, elitist stratification, and social exploitation or isolation of gifted youth that has dominated and can still dominate the DEG scene.

With these four factors in mind, the emerging DEG taxonomy with its 32 key concepts serves not only a descriptive and prescriptive role, but also a preventive function.

Table 1. Factor One: The Nature of the Gifted Learner

Theoretical Position	Subsequent Key Concepts and Recommended Practices	
	Within the framework of a multifaceted mental construct the	

The gifted learner is a cognitive type first with high degrees of intelligence and imagination. In working with the gifted learner, one must consider, however, the gifted mind on the whole. This should include not only cognitive abilities (A) but also affective (B) and conative abilities (C). This emphasis on the nonintellectual qualities of a gifted mind adds empathy and sensitivity as well as interest and motivation to the conceptual framework of this multifaceted mental construct.	*Key Concepts are:*
	 A. In the cognitive domain
	   1. Intelligence.
	   2. Imagination.
	
	 B. In the affective domain
	   1. Empathy.
	   2. Sensitivity.
	
	 C. In the conative domain
	   1. Interest.
	   2. Motivation.
		Recommended Practices are:
		 A.1. Culture-fair, individualized IQ batteries; humor scales; and standardized scholastic achievement tests.
		 A.2. Student projects and auditions.
		
		 B.1. Value inventories.
		 B.2. Attitudinal scales.
		
		 C.1. Interest inventories and motivational scales.
		 C.2. Nominational devices.

Table 2. Factor Two: The Role of the DEG Educationist

Theoretical Position	Subsequent Key Concepts and Recommended Practices	

The DEG educationist is a teacher (A), facilitator (B), and counselor (C) in working with gifted learners. In this capacity, the educationist provides not only acceleration and differentiation in content and process, but also facilitates additional resources in and out of school. Furthermore, the DEG educationist interprets the mental and personal traits of gifted learners by developing a characterology that will advance understanding of the distinguishing characteristics the gifted display.	*Key Concepts* are:
	
	A. As teacher
	  1. Acceleration.
	  2. Differentiation.
	
	B. As facilitator
	  1. Enrichment.
	  2. Leadership Training.
	
	C. As counselor
	  1. Characterology.
	  2. Mental Testing.
	  3. Restructuring.
		Within the framework of a differential pedagogy the
		
		Recommended Practices are:
		
		A.1. Transmission and acceleration of abstract contents.
		A.2. Application of differential contents, methods, and evaluations.
		
		B.1. Facilitation of parental and communal resources.
		B.2. Implementation and supervision of mentorships, internships, and/or tutorials.
		
		C.1. Development of a DEG characterology.
		C.2. Interpretation of mental tests.
		C.3. Interpretation and application of DEG personalyses.

Table 3. Factor Three: The Demands of Knowledge

Theoretical Position	Subsequent Key Concepts and Recommended Practices	Within the Frameworks of Differentiation and Articulation the
DEG is a demand for generative knowledge which places emphasis on generic and systematic structures and functions of knowledge, rather than on their factual or terminal states. Generative knowledge must lead to knowledge production which is critical for and proof of giftedness. Generativity of knowledge occurs in all content areas (A), methodology (B), and assessment (C) in order to meet the academic and developmental needs of gifted learners.	*Key Concepts are:* A. In content areas 1. Ethics. 2. Synnoetics. } DEG core 3. Synoptics. 4. Empirics. 5. Esthetics. } DEG electives 6. Symbolics. B. In methodology 1. Discovery Approach. 2. Games/Play Approach. 3. Interest Approach. 4. Polytechnical Approach. 5. Problem Approach. 6. Systems Approach. C. In assessment techniques 1. Achievement. 2. Evaluation. 3. Observation.	*Recommended Practices are:* A.1–6. Emphasis on conceptual and ideational studies in all realms of meaning. The curricular core includes ethics, synnoetics, and synoptics. The curricular electives are drawn from empirics, esthetics, and symbolics. B.1–6. Emphasis on learning how to learn, to question, to apply, and to produce knowledge responsibly, cooperatively, and independently. C.1–3. Emphasis on an achievement-oriented climate in the DEG setting that must affect not only the students but the teachers and the community at large.

Table 4. Factor Four: The Needs of Society

Theoretical Position	Subsequent Key Concepts and Recommended Practices

The DEG program must provide for the needs of a society and for the solution of its problems in an open and free atmosphere. Procedural democracy provides this framework and places emphasis on the human rights (A) and human obligations (B) of gifted learners and other members of a given community/society.	Within the framework of a free society the
	
	Key Concepts are:
	A. Concerning human rights
	  1. Democracy.
	  2. Equality.
	
	B. Concerning human obligations
	  1. Responsibility.
	  2. Responsiveness.
	
	Recommended Practices are:
	A.1. Procedural democracy as a means to safeguard against elitist or utilitarian stratification, isolation, insulation, and/or exploitation of gifted learners.
	A.2. Procedural democracy as a means to accept or reject all forms of authority that hinder or advance all forms of equality.
	
	B.1. Procedural democracy as a means to display socially responsible behavior in and out of school.
	B.2. Procedural democracy as a means to get involved in school or communal projects and problems.

Table 5. Jellen's Taxonomy[1] for DEG[2] (3rd Edition, 1984):
A Classification System of Relevant Factors, Theoretical Positions, Subsequent Key Concepts, and Recommended Practices for DEG.

Relevant Factors	Theoretical Positions	Subsequent Key Concepts	Recommended Practices
I. *The Nature of the Gifted Learner*	I. *Considering Gifted Mind on the Whole* A. Cognitive Ability. B. Affective Ability. C. Conative Ability.	I. *Within the Framework of a Multifaceted Mental Construct:* A. 1. Intelligence. 　2. Imagination. B. 1. Empathy. 　2. Sensitivity. C. 1. Interest. 　2. Motivation.	I. *Early and Valid Selection/Identification Procedures* A. 1. Culture-fair, individualized IQ batteries; humor scales; & standardized scholastic achievement tests. 　2. Student projects & auditions. B. 1. Values Inventories. 　2. Attitudinal scales. C. 1. Interest inventories & motivational scales. 　2. Nominational devices.
II. *The Role of the DEG Educationist*	II. *Considering the Trained Professional as* A. Teacher. B. Facilitator. C. Counselor.	II. *Within the Framework of a Differential Pedagogy.* A. 1. Acceleration. 　2. Differentiation. B. 1. Enrichment. 　2. Leadership Training. C. 1. Characterology. 　2. Mental Testing. 　3. Restructuring.	II. *Academic, Personal, and Social Development* A. 1. Transmission and acceleration of abstract content. 　2. Application of differential contents, methods, and evaluations. B. 1. Facilitation of parental and communal resources. 　2. Implementation and supervision of mentorships, internships, and/or tutorials. C. 1. Development of a DEG characterology. 　2. Interpretation of mental tests. 　3. Interpretation and application of DEG personalyses.
III. *The Demands of Knowledge*	III. *Considering Generativity in* A. All Content Areas. B. Methodology.	III. *Within the Frameworks of Differentiation & Articulation:* A. 1. Ethics. Curricular 　2. Synnoetics. Core. 　3. Synoptics.	III. *Knowledge Production in All Fields of Knowledge* A.1.–6.: Emphasis on conceptual and ideational studies in all realms of meaning,[3] i.e., for the curricular core (1.–3.) *and* for the curricular electives (4.–6.).

C. Assessment Techniques.

4. Empirics. Curricular
5. Esthetics. Electives.
6. Symbolics.
B. 1. Discovery Approach.
2. Games/Play Approach.
3. Interest Approach.
4. Polytechnical Approach.
5. Problem Approach.
6. Systems Approach.
C. 1. Achievement.
2. Evaluation.
3. Observation.

B.1.–6.:
Emphasis on "educere" or learning how to learn, to question, to apply, and to produce knowledge responsibly, cooperatively, and independently.
C.1.–3.:
Emphasis on an achievement-oriented climate in the DEG setting that must affect not only the students but also the teachers and the community at large.

IV. The Needs of Society

IV. *Considering the Constitutionality of a Given Society*
A. Human Rights.
B. Human Obligations.

IV. *Within the Framework of a Free Society:*
A. 1. Democracy.
2. Equality.
B. 1. Responsibility.
2. Responsiveness.

IV. *The Reproduction or Reconstruction of a Procedural Democracy*
A. 1. Procedural democracy as a means to safeguard against elitist or utilitarian stratification, isolation, insulation, and/or exploitation of gifted youth.
2. Procedural democracy as a means to accept or reject all forms of authority that hinder or advance all forms of equality.
B. 1. Procedural democracy as a means to display socially responsible behavior in and out of school.
2. Procedural democracy as a means to get involved in school or communal projects/problems.

1. Jellen's Taxonomy for DEG is an attempt to bring a knowledge base and a conceptual order to the atheoretical nature of so-called "Gifted/Talented" or "Creative Education"; see also *Gifted Education International* (1985) 3 (2): 94–99.
2. DEG or "Differential Education for the Gifted" is a term and acronym adopted from Virgil S. Ward (1981) to replace the illogical and semantic fallacy of so-called "Gifted/Talented" or "Creative Education."
3. Phenix's (1964) "Realms of Meaning" have been adopted as curricular foundation for DEG.

THE NATURE OF THE GIFTED LEARNER

KEY CONCEPTS

INTELLIGENCE

Descriptive Treatment for Intelligence

The cognitive potential of the gifted learner to develop abilities to learn abstract content fast and to criticize what is learned, as well as to deal with new and challenging situations. The gifted display high capabilities in each of these areas.

Prescriptive Treatment for Intelligence

DEG nurtures the gifted intellect by providing a differential curriculum that places emphasis on difficulty, complexity, abstractness, economy (speed), adaptiveness (flexibility), and originality.

Discussion on Intelligence

The concept of intelligence must be understood in terms of an intelligent act. An intelligent act requires concept recognition, concept formulation, concept operation, and concept application (partially adapted from Spearman, 1927, and White, 1974). Speed, flexibility, fluency, and accuracy are features of concept possession and manipulation to the extent that the conceptualizer is effectively prepared to apply or transfer his or her concept(s) in order to make connections with objects or events of the same, a similar, or a different nature (White, 1974).

DEG continues the Spearman-Terman-Eysenck tradition by studying intelligence on a dual scientific basis:

1. Through psychometric studies of individual differences.
2. Through experimental studies of the general laws of intellectual functioning (Eysenck, 1979).

The validity in assessing the Spearman paradigm (that is, the two-factor theory of intelligence) can be summarized as follows:

Data are in agreement with the proposition that all cognitive behavior is determined to varying degrees by a general innate mental ability (g) underlying all other special aptitudes and talents (s). g must be understood as a kind of weighted average or common denominator of all other primary abilities. Different persons possess g to varying degrees; giftedness is extreme positive deviation from the norm concerning g. This approach to intelligence could save DEG research a great deal of time, money, and energy since it makes the greatest contribution in our efforts to assess giftedness (Eysenck, 1979).

Centers for the gifted, as seen and understood in the context of this study, are local foci of organized and collective intelligence to help individuals or a community to cope effectively with problems and change.

See Also

Imagination; leadership training; mental testing.

Related Concepts

Ability; aptitude; capacity for learning; genius; intellect (g + s); intellectual curiosity; intelligibility; IQ; neogenesis; potential; power and sensitivity of thought; talent.

Suggested Readings

Eysenck, H. 1979. *The structure and measurement of intelligence*, 192–93. New York: Springer.

Gustafsson, E. 1981. A unifying model for the structure of intellectual abilities. *Intelligence* 8:179–203.

Spearman, C. 1927. *The abilities of man*. London: Macmillan.

Undheim, J. 1981. On intelligence IV: Toward a restoration of general intelligence. *Scandinavian Journal of Psychology* 22: 251–65.

White, J. 1974. Intelligence and the logic of the nature-nurture issue. In *Proceedings of the Philosophy of Education Society of Great Britain*, eds. Peters et. al, 3 (1): 30–51.

IMAGINATION

Descriptive Treatment for Imagination

The mental ability and power to recombine things from past experiences into a new pattern of images. (Images are mental copies of something not present to the senses.) Because of the high imagination the gifted display, DEG encourages these learners to create their own new and unique meanings of objects and events.

Prescriptive Treatment for Imagination

DEG must allow gifted learners to create their own meaning and interpretations of objects or events and to explore the unfamiliar, mysterious, or unknown. Encouragement to ascribe the new meanings in the objects or situations before them is required in DEG in order to achieve originality and creativity.

Discussion on Imagination

Arieti (1976) points out that images are microinnovations of becoming. They liberate the innovative mind from punctilious reproduction of reality. Imagination is, therefore, a mental representation of something the mind wants to be by creating an inner surrogate of the outside world. Arieti sees image production as the true building block for innovative and productive thinking.

DEG accepts this view by incorporating Spearman's g factor of intelligence in order to understand imagination. Terman, too, supports this notion by stating that "creativity" has to be backed by a high degree of g especially in those considered genius (Terman, 1954, p. 224). In genius, nature synthesized intelligence and imagination (Arieti, 1976).

DEG is very critical, however, of so-called "creativity training" and "creative problem solving." Even though this nomenclature dominates the contemporary DEG literature, research findings are too meager to provide grounds for optimism that such learning packages will ever affect innovative and original thought (that is, knowledge production) on a professional scale (Mansfield, et al., 1978). DEG is much more interested in creating a learning climate that allows for autonomy of thought and action. Gifted students are asked to make their own attempts to interpret and to share what they conceive to be symbolically significant. They are also encouraged to reformulate what they know to be "true" in alternative terms. DEG involves the educationist and the gifted learner in a kind of intellectual humility by emphasizing probabilities rather than certainties, and an imaginative awareness or awe that problems get more complex rather than more simplistic the more one knows about them (McKellar, 1957, p. 194).

See Also

Discovery Approach; games/play approach; intelligence.

Related Concepts

Appearance (from within); altruism (A-thinking); awe; concretization; creativity; daydreaming; fantasy; hallucination; imagery; impression(s); interpretation; originality; perception; probability; productive thinking (R-thinking); surrealism; symbolism; vision; wonder.

Suggested Readings

Arieti, S. 1976. *Creativity: The magic synthesis*. New York: Basic Books.

Mansfield, B. et al. 1978. The effectiveness of creativity training. *Review of Educational Research* 48 (4): 517–36.

McKellar, P. 1957. *Imagination and thinking*, 194. London: Cohen and West.

Terman, L. 1954. The discovery and encouragement of exceptional talent. *The American Psychologist* 9: 224ff.

EMPATHY

Descriptive Treatment for Empathy

The identification with the interests, attitudes, and feeling of another person or group, thereby inducing feeling of being as one with the other person or persons. The empathic feeling is developed from *intellectual* knowledge of the person or persons as a result of the DEG program.

Prescriptive Treatment for Empathy

DEG cultivates acceptance and understanding of self and others in the gifted learner through the development of reasons and compassion and not through a purely emotive or subjective response. It also reinforces processes of self-regulation and self-control of empathically aroused affect.

Discussion on Empathy

Functional empathy (altruism) is seen as a vital social skill to be developed in prospective leaders, reformers, innovators, and problem solvers. Failure to take the role of another person must be interpreted as a sign of egocentricity, which demands special attention and cognitive restructuring (Trower et al., 1978).

Mature empathy implies an awareness and understanding of the fact that the source of one's affection resides in a sense of what the other person is feeling (Hoffman, 1978). The gifted child must learn to interpret and identify this agitated state of affective operations in terms of the characteristics of a given situation and his own apperception he brings to the event (Schachter and Singer, 1962). This *cognitive* component of empathy enables him or her to transform the victim's actual distress into a more reciprocal feeling of concern with a genuine desire to relieve the distress perceived in the other person (Hoffman, 1978).

Further, empathic development is necessary to motivate altruistic behavior on a broader scale. This implies comprehending the plight not only of one's fellow man but also of an entire group or class of people who are economically impoverished, politically oppressed, social outcasts, victims of terror or war, mentally retarded, or socially handicapped (Hoffman, 1978, pp. 238–47). The highest and probably the least frequent form of empathy is that in which the gifted individual is compelled to embrace all human beings regardless of race, color, creed, sex, or economic status.

Biographical studies of people with high levels of functional empathty, acting in accordance with genuine efforts to better humanity (for example, Schweitzer or Mother Theresa), may trigger desired self-examination and restructuring of values not only in the gifted child but in the DEG educationist as well.

See Also

Ethics; leadership training; restructuring; sensitivity.

Related Concepts

Acceptance; arousal (empathetic); attitude; awareness (of self and others); benevolence; compassion; compunction; emotivity; friendliness; guilt; identification; pity; prosocial action; reciprocal concern; sensitivity; sentiment; sympathy; understanding.

Suggested Readings

Clark, K. 1980. Empathy: A neglected topic in psychological research. *American Psychologist* 35 (2): 187–90.
Hoffman, M. 1979. Toward a theory of empathic arousal and development. In *The development of affect,* eds. Lewis and Rosenblum, 238–47. New York: Plenum.

SENSITIVITY

Descriptive Treatment for Sensitivity

The tendency of detecting, and of being easily moved by, sense stimuli or emotive situations, whether pleasant or unpleasant. Gifted learners display high degrees of sensitivity toward self and others in group or individual situations.

Prescriptive Treatment for Sensitivity

Sensitivity is a social skill which must receive attention in DEG. DEG must apply group techniques or individual counseling designed to achieve a balance between autistic (self-serving) and altruistic (other-serving) behavior. Increasing awareness of how both behaviors affect self and others is critical to the restructuring process of the gifted learner.

Discussion on Sensitivity

The starting point of any analysis of the growth of sensitivity must be the fact that all social knowledge implies taking the viewpoint of another person or group of persons. The standpoint of others provides a platform for getting outside oneself in order to acknowledge and to understand differences. Self- and social awareness are developed through social interaction, which implies that one may know oneself only to the extent that one knows others (Light, 1979).

The mechanism through which the gifted individual becomes able and sensitive enough to view himself as a socialized being is that of role taking. Role taking in DEG is seen as a prototypical social-cognitive skill, by which the learner does not just take the role of the other but enters into the perspective of the other person. It is a *cognitive* process of taking account of another point of view. In this sense, then, role taking is perspective taking with a gradual awareness of the diversity of perspectives in a situation in which the learner and others are involved (Light, 1979). It requires from the student and his or her educationist a delay of overt action, while surveying the meanings and consequences of proposed acts in terms of others' probable responses (Mead, 1964).

The role played by the gifted child is one of interpreting data furnished to him or her in such social settings as "boundary breaking," "values clarification," "group encounter," and "simulation games." All of these socialization strategies should reinforce the student's role as a self-conscious actor by teaching him or her not only to assume multiple positions vis-à-vis himself or herself, but also by teaching him or her to organize these positions into a system of *cognitive* schemata. The very quality of his thought, feelings, and drives is seen as reflecting the quality of experienced social interaction (that is, the gifted learner being able to communicate effectively with others who do not share an identical perspective).

See Also

Empathy; leadership training; observation; restructuring.

Related Concepts

Affectibility; awareness (of self and others); self-awareness as subject and self-awareness as social subject; sensibility; sensitivity; sensitization; sentiment(s); socialization; socialized individualism.

Suggested Readings

Light, P. 1979. *The development of social sensitivity*, 8–10, 109. Cambridge, England: Cambridge University Press.

Mead, G. 1964. *On social psychology*, xxiii. Chicago: Phoenix Books.

INTEREST

Descriptive Treatment for Interest

A freely chosen activity which holds the attention and is a source of satisfaction or pleasure to the gifted learner. In DEG learner interests may be revealed by an interest inventory.

Prescriptive Treatment for Interest

The dimensions of learners' interests considered for DEG research, theory, and practice include their duration, extensity, and intensity. Duration indicates how long certain interests persist; extensity addresses the total range of the gifted learner's interests; and intensity shows preference for one interest over another. Most interest inventories given to gifted learners reveal a preference for intellectually challenging types of activities over repetitive and redundant types.

Discussion on Interest

Terman's (1925) and Hollingworth's (1942) studies of gifted learners draw attention to the wide range and versatility of the learners' interests. Such activities as intensive reading, collecting of objects, and building models seem to reoccur as dominant interest areas of the gifted throughout the investigations of the two scholars. All of these activities involve concentrated thinking and long-term planning on part of the gifted learner. The more gifted a child, the more likely he or she is to be a self-starter on any of these interest activities that involve concentration and persistence over a long period of time.

DEG encourages, supports, and constructively guides the interests of the gifted and their enthusiasm in learning what *they* are interested in while the interest lasts. Special efforts are made to bring out specific interests directed toward isolated objects, activities, or subjects. Team work and cooperation are stressed by building on common interests of the gifted group (cf. interest approach).

Since DEG is also interested in personal and vocational guidance, educational interest tests and inventories are used in helping gifted students select appropriate curricula and professional careers. The scores of the instruments assess mechanical, computational, scientific, persuasive, artistic, literary, musical, social-service, and clerical interests. From these scores inferences can be made regarding student interest as a starting point for programmatic DEG enrichment as well as guidance for specific occupations. Research and guidance in interests might make it possible for genius to emerge and to flourish early (Berdie, 1946).

See Also

Interest approach; motivation.

Related Concepts

Attention; attraction; choice; disliking; liking; persistence; preference; preferential hierarchy.

Suggested Readings

Berdie, R. 1946. Interests. In *Encyclopedia of psychology*, ed. Harriman, 305–14. New York: Philosophical Library.

Hollingworth, L. 1942. *Children above 180 IQ*. New York: Harcourt & Brace.

Terman, L. 1925. *Genetic studies of genius (vol. I): Mental and physical traits of a thousand gifted children*. Stanford, CA: Stanford University Press.

MOTIVATION

Descriptive Treatment for Motivation

The process of arousing, sustaining, and regulating learning activities in gifted learners by having them work for a prize rather than for satisfaction in the task itself (extrinsic) or by having them receive satisfaction or incentive conditions that are derived from within the activity itself (intrinsic). DEG reinforces both forms of motivation in gifted learners.

Prescriptive Treatment for Motivation

The guidance of motivational dynamics in the gifted learner is critical to the DEG program. Inciting and effecting academic, personal, and social development through one's own drive and initiative results in a desire to learn, to grow, and to be productive throughout life. The lifelong education of the gifted learner is based on early recognition of vision and mission in his or her lifetime. DEG must fulfill this important visionary and missionary role in gifted learners.

Discussion on Motivation

Innovators, inventors, composers, and reformers (that is, knowledge producers) seem to be endowed with strong motivational qualities involving a degree of resoluteness and egotism that sustains them in their productive endeavors. They also seem to be almost indifferent to the feat of making mistakes and to social disapproval. They have a sense of destiny and mission, an unshakable belief in the worth and validity of their efforts that helps them overcome frustrations, obstacles, and often social ridicule. Knowledge production (KP) does, therefore, not only depend on cognition, but also on the conative or motivational aspects of a gifted personality (Dallas and Gaier, 1975, p. 198).

It is motivation that serves as a catalyst and dynamic for productive and original thinking. DEG seeks out and reinforces such motivational factors as drive, dedication to work, interests, resourcefulness, strive for general principles and systems, drive to bring order to disorder, desire to bridge epistemological gaps, and willingness to discover, to explore, and to risk (Taylor, 1964).

Motivational linkages for success or achievement are: ability-competence, confidence, effort-relaxation, others-gratitude, and luck-surprise. For failure and underachievement the motivational associations are: ability-incompetence, effort-guilt, shame, others–anger, and no luck–surprise (Weiner, 1980, p. 5). These causal relationships residing within (for example, confidence) or outside the gifted learner (for instance, teacher reward) can be associated with self-esteem and self-worth. DEG makes special efforts to elicit both without falling prey to low expectancy of standards and success. Student-initiated and student-executed activities increase motivation dramatically when dealing with the gifted learner's interest areas.

See Also

Achievement; interest; interest approach.

Related Concepts

Achievement; aspiration; conation; creativity; curiosity; drive; enthusiasm; interest; risk taking; self-actualization; volition; will.

Suggested Readings

Dellas, M., and E. Gaier. 1975. Identification of creativity: The individual. In *Psychology and education of the gifted*, eds. Barbe and Renzulli, 2nd ed., 195–97. New York: Irvington.

Gefferth, E. 1981. Motivation in the background of mathematical talent. *Pszichologia* 2: 243–69.

Taylor, C. and J. Holland. 1964. Predictors of creative performance. In *Creativity: Progress and potential*, ed. Taylor. New York: McGraw-Hill.

Weiner, B. 1980. The role of affect in rational (attributional) approaches to human motivation. *Educational Researcher* 9 (7): 4–11.

THE ROLE OF THE DEG EDUCATIONIST

Key Concepts

A.1   Acceleration
A.2   Differentiation

B.1   Enrichment
B.2   Leadership Training

C.1   Characterology
C.2   Mental Testing
C.3   Restructuring

ACCELERATION

Descriptive Treatment for Acceleration

The process whereby a gifted learner makes educational progress faster than usual, whether measured by advancement in school grade or by actual achievement. DEG must provide a range of opportunities for acceleration to all gifted learners in order to free them from the academic lock-step approach that seems to permeate the climate of normal or traditional schooling.

Prescriptive Treatment for Acceleration

Administrative or parental decisions are required to move the gifted learner through normal school more rapidly than usual. These practices may include: early admission; grade skipping; advanced placement; telescoping of grade levels; credit by examination; taking correspondence courses; assigning special mentor(s)/tutor(s); and going to special school(s) or class(es).

Discussion on Acceleration

Acceleration is a form of programmatic enrichment in DEG that addresses rapid growth of idiographic know-how, especially in the cognitive domain. Accelerative enrichment is traditionally based on administrative and parental consent as a means of nurturing specific aptitudes (for instance, mathematics or music). Only a few selected cases can be made against accelerated forms of instruction and learning in DEG. Greater harm is done in the personal development of gifted children by refusal to let them move ahead. Terman (1954) illustrates this point supportively by maintaining that "the facts obtained in the thirty-year follow-up of our large, gifted group prove conclusively that children of 135 IQ or higher, who are accelerated one, two, or even three years, are usually more successful in later life than equally bright children who are held in lockstep" (pp. 230–52). It is recommended, however, to involve the gifted learner in plotting the accelerated progression of his own education.

See Also

Enrichment; intelligence.

Related Concepts

Ability and aptitudinal training; intellectual precocity; study of mathematically precocious youth (SMPY); training of talent; vertical enrichment.

Suggested Readings

Pressey, S. 1949. *Educational acceleration: Appraisals and basic problems*. Columbus, OH: Ohio State University Press.

Stanley, J. 1973. Accelerating the educational progress of intellectually gifted youth. *Educational Psychologist* 10:133–46.

Terman, L., and M. Oden. 1954. Major issues in the education of the gifted child. *Journal of Technical Education* 5: 230–52.

Ward, V. 1980. *Differential education for the gifted*, 35–36. Los Angeles: National/State Leadership Training Institute on the Gifted and Talented.

DIFFERENTIATION

Descriptive Treatment for Differentiation

A plan for meeting individual differences in gifted learners. The contents, methods, and evaluations chosen for DEG differ in degree of difficulty, range of student interests, quantity and quality of content, as well as timing in order to meet the gifted learner's academic and developmental needs.

Prescriptive Treatment for Differentiation

Educational and other growth experiences must be developed that are uniquely or predominantly suited for the distinguishing behavioral processes of intellectually superior gifted learners and the adult roles that they typically assume as leaders, innovators, writers, composers, and/or reformers—in short, as knowledge producers.

Discussion on Differentiation

Differentiation is primarily concerned with epistemological content and pedagogical method. DEG directs its efforts to provide differentially for children who are differentially endowed with intellectual, emotional, and volitional ability. Differentation provides, therefore, an elevated or transformed plane of experience (that is, a meta-curriculum) involving higher levels of learning and thinking. Qualitative characteristics of a differential experience should address curricular and methodological considerations of a different sort.

1. *Education for Life Span*
   All educational experience should be planned as integral to the development of the whole person and to the entire life career of the individual.

2. *Development of Aptitudes*
   The identification and nurture of peak behavioral potential without falling prey to early specialization.
3. *Education for Reconstruction*
   Methodological studies (methods and research on learning how to learn) in any field of knowledge contributing to knowledge production and procedural know-how (that is, problem solving).
4. *Education for Leadership*
   Preparation and training for leadership in the democratic context. A willingness to share useful knowledge with others.
5. *Differential Epistemological Content*
   a. "Extensification" or "horizontal enrichment" implies additional learning experiences in those curricular areas that are not covered in normal schooling and that have generative value (for example, in symbolics: applied logic, linguistics, statistics, and computer science).
   b. "Intensification" or "vertical enrichment" deals with functional concepts, summary analyses, hidden realities, significant theses, or great ideas within a given content area.
6. *Differential Pedagogical Methodology*
   a. "Educare" implies the disciplining of a gifted mind. The shifting from fact getting (that is, knowledge consumption) to fact finding and independent research (knowledge utilization). It focuses on a different kind of discourse that is essentially theoretical, abstract, and problematic.
   b. "Educere" addresses the leading out of giftedness. An effort should be made to reverse the ratio between the amount of teaching and the amount of self-learning or discovery. The shifting from fact finding and independent research (knowledge utilization) to ideational discovery (knowledge production) is important. (Partially adapted from Ward et al., 1962, pp. 61–66).

See Also

Appendix C; enrichment.

Related Concepts

DEG (Differential Education for the Gifted)

Suggested Readings

Ward, V. et al. 1962. *The gifted student: A manual for program improvement*, 61–66. Atlanta: Southern Regional Education Board.

Ward, V. 1980. *Differential education for the gifted*, 86–101. Los Angeles: National/State Leadership Training Institute of the Gifted and Talented.

Enrichment

Descriptive Treatment of Enrichment

The process of selective modification of existing curricular experiences by exploring content areas not ordinarily covered in normal schools (horizontal enrichment); or the offering of advanced work in order to achieve early specialization (vertical enrichment). DEG deliberately enriches the curriculum by challenging and developing gifted learners' intellectual, emotional, moral, and social capabilities.

Prescriptive Treatment of Enrichment

DEG must provide for both horizontal and vertical enrichment on a programmatic basis. Programmatic enrichment for the gifted should not supplant but supplement the curricular offerings of normal schooling by systematically and deliberately increasing the breadth and depth of the gifted learner's educational experiences to be based on sound articulation and differentiation.

Discussion on Enrichment

Programmatic enrichment of both the horizontal and vertical nature intends to give gifted students differential educative experiences based on generative knowledge. These experiences can be gained both in and out of school. But curriculum and pedagogy must indicate logic, sequence, and design for a meaningful enrichment program to emerge. The logic for programmatic enrichment asserts that the superior abilities characteristic of the gifted should be related through the educative process to the probable role of reconstruction and leadership which will be thrusted upon the gifted individual (Ward, 1980, p. 85). Sequence addresses a comprehensive scheme of educational and developmental experiences which the average or below-average child lacks the time, interest, and intellect to understand and to appreciate. A good DEG design extends the gifted child's sphere of activity from the classroom into the total school program and the community or society at large.

A sound enrichment program for the gifted also meets the needs of individual differences and includes such practices as allowing individual plans to substitute for group enterprises; allowing initiative in the pursuit of a project when a perspective is established with respect to purposes and goals; granting freedom to move along the lines of the educative design at any rate of speed commensurate with optimum gain; giving permission to vary the depth of exploration with different curricular segments; affording a flexible evaluation of all the endeavors within a given period; and allowing some free time unstructured by assignments and unfettered by the design itself, so that the uniqueness of the personality may achieve expression (Ward, 1980, p. 101).

Havighurst et al. (1955) list several points which have been slightly modified here and which cover the essentials of programmatic enrichment in DEG.

1. Emphasis on intellectual and experimental activities.
2. Independent work or group work, involving student planning.
3. Reinforcement of high standards and task commitment.
4. Tutorials from experts and firsthand experiences.
5. A genuine concern for community responsibility (Havighurst et al. in Vernon, 1977, p. 180).

See Also

Appendix C; differentiation; leadership training.

Related Concepts

DEG; enrichment triad; programmatic enrichment (sequenced learning); provisional enrichment (non-sequential, ad hoc, or randomly chosen learning experiences).

Suggested Readings

Vernon, P. et al. 1977. *The psychology and education of gifted children*, 172–96. London: Methuen.

Ward, V. 1980. *Differential education for the gifted*, 85 and 101. Los Angeles: National/State Leadership Training Institute on the Gifted and Talented.

Leadership Training

Descriptive Treatment for Leadership Training

The processing of the ability and readiness of gifted learners to inspire, guide, and/or manage others in and out of school. DEG develops leadership in the gifted as well as in DEG educationists.

Prescriptive Treatment for Leadership Training

DEG must offer teachers and learners opportunities to develop leadership skills, to practice group process, to reinforce self-initiative, to make democratic decisions, and, finally, to consider all the consequences before taking action. For the DEG educationist, leadership training is required through in-service and formal university training and applies to teachers, administrators, and auxiliary personnel directly or indirectly involved in DEG.

Discussion on Leadership Training

Both the DEG educationist and the gifted learner must understand procedural democracy first before democratic leadership can emerge. Procedural democracy is a form of checks and balances in which authority is given a rational procedure, in which liberty safeguards free discussion and assembly, and in which accountability is embedded in the practices of a people. This form of governing represents the only form of political life or leadership that is consistent with the fundamental principles of social ethics (Peters, 1966). Under such conditions, DEG becomes an exemplary form of democratic life, a miniature community of collective intelligence, and a model for situational leadership. All of these facets must operate on morally justifiable grounds.

It is a sociological tenet of DEG that, as a form of special education, it can only be justified on democratic grounds when it becomes a means to emphasize, to develop, and to share procedural know-how effectively with other schools, citizens, minorities, and the community at large. The sharing of knowledge is a social responsibility that safeguards against elitist stratification and isolation of gifted youth. DEG must, therefore, produce democratic leadership that reflects a genuine concern for others and a willingness to take civic responsibility. Social reconstructionism or DEG leadership asserts that an interest in learning and sharing of knowledge from all aspects of life is essential to the survival of procedural democracy in a given society.

In order to solve problems and to settle differences democratically, democratic leadership encourages matters of conflict to be resolved by recourse to reasonable discussion and the application of collective intelligence rather than by recourse to force or arbitrary and authoritarian ideology (Peters, 1966).

See Also

Democracy; empathy; ethics; interest approach; polytechnical approach; sensitivity.

Related Concepts

For the DEG educationist: in-service training; leadership training institute; model demonstration projects; preservice training; workshops.

For the gifted learner: boldness; drive; energy; ethics; group awareness; responsibility; risk taking; strategy; volition.

Suggested Readings

Magoon, R., and H. Jellen. 1980. *Educational strategies: Leadership development—democracy in action.* Poquoson, VA: Human Development Press.

Peters, R. S. 1966. *Ethics in education.* London: Allen and Unwin.

Characterology

Descriptive Treatment for Characterology

The process which attempts to estimate the character, temperament, physical stamina, and mental ability of the gifted learner. The DEG educationist must afford training in this neglected area in order to gain illuminating data on the traits and characteristics of the gifted learner.

Prescriptive Treatment for Characterology

DEG advocates the scientific study of the organization of cognitive, affective, and conative traits that contribute to a gifted learner's character. Every facet of gifted behavior must be explored and recorded by the educationist in order to confirm or refute hypotheses about giftedness. Data gathering and data interpretation in DEG must include: case histories; diaries; ratings; biographies; correspondence; introspection; inventories; questionnaires; clinical records; personalyses; psychoanalyses; clues from such expressive behaviors as art, drama, fiction, and/or music; as well as experimentation and intuition. This form of inquiry in DEG has the greatest potential in making DEG a science in education.

Discussion on Characterology

Studies of personality are studies of humans in general. Studies of character address personality as it reveals itself in differentiated human beings (Roback, 1952, p. 499). Characterology in DEG focuses on characteristics or differential modes of behavior that distinguish the gifted from the general populace. It is the study of human behavior with regard to what is characteristically gifted.

Mind (that is, cognition, affect, and conation) is particularly relevant to DEG research in its pursuit of establishing a typology of giftedness. Body is another consideration for characterology. The handbook distinguishes characterology ("what is") from ethical studies ("what ought to be"), since character presupposes the existence of values. The precedence of ethics is undertaken as a separate study in DEG but is paralleled by research in the psychology of cognition, affect, and conation. Both ethical studies and characterology are seen as the stage for the "training and taming" of the will by aiding DEG educationists in the formulation of behavioral content (that is, ethical studies) and behavioral form (that is, cognitive restructuring).

Personalysis in characterology cannot but assist DEG educators in bringing out the differences of certain qualities of gifted behavior that are generally treated as if they were identical or nonexistent (for instance, affect and conation).

See Also

Observation; restructuring.

Related Concepts

The scientific study of: human characteristics, constitution, giftedness, individuality, interest(s), judgment, motivation, nature, qualities, talents, traits, types, uniqueness, will, and willingness.

Suggested Readings

Allport, G. 1937. *Personality: A psychological interpretation*. New York: Holt.

Gerth, H., and C. Mills. 1953. *Character and social structure*. New York: Harcourt, Brace, and World.

McCormick, L. 1920. *Characterology: An exact science*. New York: Rand McNally.

Roback, A. 1952. *The psychology of character*, 3rd ed., 160, 499, 543–44. London: Routledge and Kegan.

Mental Testing

Descriptive Treatment for Mental Testing

The determination of the strength of various mental abilities of gifted learners and DEG educationists as assessed by some standardized measure. In DEG, mental testing is critical in order to assess objectively the performance of gifted learners and DEG educationists.

Prescriptive Treatment for Mental Testing

Psychometric devices for the fair identification and selection of gifted learners from all socio-ethnic and socio-economic backgrounds are required. Fair identification must involve the use of multifaceted, valid, and reliable criteria to assess giftedness as a mental construct rather than as a single mental concept with focus on the intellectual as well as nonintellectual qualities of a gifted mind.

Discussion on Mental Testing

DEG uses mental tests for three reasons:
1. To provide more accurate descriptions of gifted students and their behavior.
2. To assist DEG personnel in making decisions about the gifted in terms of
   a. selection for DEG programs
   b. identification for aptitudinal studies within a DEG program
   c. recommendation for a particular form of educational-vocational enrichment and psychological counseling.
3. To help administrative personnel in making decisions about DEG staff concerning

a. selection for a DEG program
b. identification for in-service training
c. recommendation for a particular position with regards to educational ability or psychological expertise (partially adapted from: Annett, 1974)

DEG insists upon the use of several identification instruments and processes such as individual but culture-fair IQ tests, aptitudinal tests, achievement tests, tests to assess imaginative ability, interest inventories, personality scales, motivational indicators, and performance auditions. A composite of all scores should be the deciding factor of whether a student will be invited to attend a DEG enrichment program or not. Flexibility must be shown, however, when dealing with disadvantaged and minority children.

Intelligence (that is, high g saturation) as indexed by culture-fair IQ tests remains, however, the most important single quality that promises success in the objective identification of giftedness (Eysenck, 1979, p. 101). Testing gifted students regularly on an annual basis is essential to obtaining a personalysis of giftedness that has empirical backing.

See Also

Appendix D and observation.

Related Concepts

Achievement tests; aptitude tests; attitude surveys; creativity tests; intelligence tests; interest inventories; observation (ethology); personality tests; rating scales.

Suggested Readings

Annett, J., ed. 1974. *Psychometrics*, 125. Milton Keynes, England: The Open Univ. Press.
Buros, O., ed. 1980. *The eighth mental measurements yearbook*. Vols. 1 and 2. Highland Park, NJ: Gryphon Press.
Eysenck, H. 1979. *The structure and measurement of intelligence*, 101. New York: Springer.

Restructuring

Descriptive Treatment for Restructuring

The process of making a fundamental change in the cognitive set of gifted learners. DEG assists the gifted by providing them with alternatives conducive to living successful, productive, and enjoyable lives in a given community/society.

Prescriptive Treatment for Restructuring

Cognitive restructuring in DEG should assist the gifted learner in discovering and ferreting out self-defeating behaviors by substituting constructive and sensible alternatives to rational living. DEG must help to reduce the gifted's vulnerability and to develop forms of coping with the realities of life.

Discussion on Restructuring

The maturational concept of restructuring acknowledges the gifted mind, on the whole, but focuses on the cognitive component of mental behavior in order to elicit attitudinal change. Cognitive restructuring is a therapeutic facet of DEG to correct the misconceptions gifted learners might have about themselves, others, and their environment.

DEG conducts special "values sessions" to replace dichotomous reasoning (good-bad, right-wrong, black-white, and so forth) which frequently leads to overgeneralizations and prejudice, with nonjudgmental forms of analytical thinking. It is assumed that understanding and insight are changes in cognition that may lead to changes in behavior (Lazarus, 1971, p. 165).

The application of collective intelligence (that is, the analysis and discussion of problems in group sessions) increases rationality with regard to the number of alternatives available. The quoting of relevant parables, metaphors, and analogies from "wise" individuals is an effective way to restructure attitudes found in dogma or irrational belief systems. These citations and discussions must bring clarity to problematic situations that are related to a gifted person's own experience in living. The purpose is to achieve a fitting detachment from arbitrary dogma, which only limits human happiness and mars the pursuit of a rich and joyful life (Lazarus, 1971, p. 176).

If this form of maturational therapy (Ellis, 1961), adopted for the gifted, is to have any enduring value, it should communicate to them the full meaning of social or personal change and should also heighten their concern for the improvement of culture and life itself.

See Also

Characterology; empathy; ethics; leadership training; problem approach; sensitivity.

Related Concepts

Behavior therapy; cognitive restructuring; rational-emotive psychotherapy; self-knowledge; theory of positive personal constructs.

Suggested Readings

Ellis, A., and R. Harper. 1961. *A guide to rational living*. Englewood Cliffs, NJ: Prentice-Hall.

Lazarus, A. 1971. *Behavior therapy and beyond*, 163–84. New York: McGraw-Hill.

Raths, L. et al. 1978. *Values and teaching*. 2nd ed. Columbus, OH: Merril.

Simon, S. et al. 1978. *Values clarification*. New York: Visual Library.

The Demands of Knowledge
Key Concepts

A.1. Ethics   ⎫
A.2. Synnoetics ⎬ for a DEG-core
A.3. Synoptics ⎭

A.4. Empirics   ⎫
A.5. Esthetics   ⎬ for DEG-electives
A.6. Symbolics ⎭

B.1. Discovery Approach
B.2. Games/Play Approach
B.3. Interest Approach
B.4. Polytechnical Approach
B.5. Problem Approach
B.6. Systems Approach

C.1. Achievement
C.2. Evaluation
C.3. Observation

Ethics

Descriptive Treatment for Ethics

The branch of philosophy concerned with morals and the distinction between right and wrong, or good and evil. DEG familiarizes the gifted learner with moral principles and forms of moral reasoning.

Prescriptive Treatment for Ethics

Ethics in DEG is prescribed for gifted learners not only for them to acquire knowledge (for example, philosophy, ethics, religion), skills (for instance, altruism), and modes of conduct (for example, cooperation), but also for them to acquire these moral contents, skills, and modes in a manner that involves understanding and evaluating the rationale underlying them through scientific methods. The rigorous application of scientific method should be the cornerstone of moral education.

Discussion on Ethics

The essence of this study is the systematic training in good conduct. The touchstone of good conduct is to be found in religions, educational traditions, national culture, and empirics about human nature (Wall, 1974). Therefore, DEG draws its theoretical codification for ethical studies from the following four areas that can be associated with culture, customs, and traditions: (1) Christianity and Judaisim, (2) pragmatism, (3) democracy, and (4) empirics. Christianity and Judaism offer a sense of striving for perfection, a belief in the sacredness of human life, and a certain amount of empathy toward our fellow human beings (Peter, 1973). Pragmatism encourages problem solving and the production of useful knowledge according to personal and societal demands. Democracy allows for the kind of freedom that is necessary to engage in critical discussion and rational debate in order to overcome personal differences; it also ensures social growth and tolerance for others. Empirics instruct the DEG educationist and the gifted learner in the pursuit of objectivity, relevance, and mental discipline. Studies in the psychological nature of moral motives or an analysis of duties and rules in a given society in connection with social institutions and customs provide enough content to foster maturation in synnoetics (that is, personal insight about oneself and society on the whole).

These areas of substantive content can contribute together to a moral theory for DEG that can maintain consistency between the ethical ideal and the practical act. The study of ethics in DEG should result in autonomous individuals acting according to principles that have universal value; furthermore, this study should reinforce the strong will needed to enact those values.

The DEG educationist must introduce certain "generic concepts" and "great ideas" essential to the realm of ethics. Generic concepts that should be known and understood by all gifted learners include autonomy, custom and convention, desire, drive, free will, habit, interest, motivation, pleasure, pain, and religion(s). Great ideas with which the gifted learner should grapple are duty, God, good and evil, justice, principle, right and wrong, salvation, sin, vice, and virtue.

See Also

Characterology; democracy; empathy; restructuring; synnoetics.

Related Concepts

Conation; insight; religiosity; volition.

Suggested Readings

Havighurst, R. J., and H. Taba. 1949. *Adolescent character and personality*. New York: John Wiley and Sons.
Hollingworth, L. S. 1926. *Gifted children, their nature and nurture*. New York: Macmillan.

Phenix, P. 1964. *Realms of meaning*, 213–32. New York: McGraw-Hill.

Ward, V. 1980. *Differential education for the gifted*, 181–222. Los Angeles: National/State Leadership Training Institute on the Gifted and Talented.

SYNNOETICS

Descriptive Treatment for Synnoetics

Personal or social knowledge that is concrete, direct, existential, and necessary to understand oneself and others. Synnoetic meanings are reflectively elaborated on and expressed in psychology, sociology, philosophy, religion, and works of literature that portray the uniquely personal and social dimensions of knowledge producers.

Prescriptive Treatment for Synnoetics

Synnoetic knowledge may apply to oneself, others, or things. Thus DEG should engage the gifted learner in the analysis and evaluation of intrapersonal and interpersonal relationships. DEG must focus on a balanced growth of personhood, that is, a harmonious development of cognition, affect, and conation.

Discussion on Synnoetics

Gaining personal and social knowledge in DEG is necessary to learn how to think as an authentic and socially responsible person. Synnoetics in DEG helps the gifted learner realize that managing human relationships presupposes acknowledgment, acceptance, and also sacrifice in those relationships.

Effective teaching in the realm of synnoetics requires extraordinary insight into the profound depths of a gifted mind. Meaning lies in the personal and social comprehension of a set of particulars that will help the gifted to understand and utilize their exceptionalities constructively. Knowledge Production (KP) in synnoetics implies the ability of the gifted student to project human relatedness to a level of sophistication different from the norm. In this context, the gifted must be able not only to understand and accept themselves and others, but must also be willing to improve the quality of human life. It is the role of the DEG educationist to introduce the gifted learner in synnoetics to such "generic concepts" as actualization, affection, belongingness, commitment, compassion, custom, empathy, esteem, giftedness, insight, needs, openness, peace, security, sensitivity, and trust. "Great ideas" must include authenticity, autonomy, being and becoming, culture, enlightenment, freedom, fulfillment, love, respect, safety, and tolerance.

See Also

Characterology; leadership training; responsibility; responsiveness; restructuring.

Related Concepts

Existential awareness; hierarchy of needs; personal/social knowledge; relational insight.

Suggested Readings

Buber, M. 1958. *I and thou*. New York: Charles Scribner's Sons.

Heilbroner, R. 1974. *An inquiry into the human prospect*. New York: W. Norton.

Phenix, P. 1964. *Realms of meaning*, 186–226. New York: McGraw-Hill.

Polanyi, M. 1958. *Personal knowledge*. Chicago: University of Chicago Press.

Ward, V. 1980. *Differential education for the gifted*. 31–32, 41–47, and 108–17. Los Angeles: National/State Leadership Training Institute on the Gifted and Talented.

SYNOPTICS

Descriptive Treatment for Synoptics

Meaning that is comprehensively integrated through the disciplines of history, religion, and philosophy in order to form a whole. DEG encourages gifted learners to think in terms of broad concepts and a variety of facts pertinent to achieve a comprehensive perspective on the creation and evolution of life and cosmos.

Prescriptive Treatment for Synoptics

DEG should utilize history, religion, and philosophy in order to synthesize these various essential meanings into a comprehensive whole that must lead to a defensible philosophy for life.

Discussion on Synoptics

Through historical interpretation, the gifted learner and the DEG educationist will engage in a critical reconstruction of the past. Such a study will result in an understanding of the significant events in the history of humanity, the choices made by people in the context of given circumstances, and the individuals who have shaped human culture, particularly those deemed worthy or unworthy as role models for the gifted. Through a study of religion, the gifted learner and the educationist will explore ultimate meanings in the context of spirituality, considering, in the process, the concepts of the Whole, the Comprehensive, and the Transcendent. Through a study of philosophy, the gifted learner and the educationist will engage in conceptual analysis, evaluation, and synthesis of all realms of meaning in their differences and interrelationships. Knowledge production (KP) will be comprised of having formulated a conceptual foundation that represents a defensible philosophy for life.

The DEG educationist must introduce the following "generic concepts" essential to the realm of synoptics: life and death, humanity, metaphysics, nature, theology, and time. "Great ideas" with which the gifted learner must grapple are: being, chance, dialectic, eternity, fate, God, ideals, immortality, mind, necessity and contingency, one and the many, progress, same and the other, soul, truth, the universal and the particular, and wisdom.

See Also

Leadership training; restructuring; systems approach.

Related Concepts

History; philosophy; religion.

Suggested Readings

Hutchins, R. M. 1952. Preface to *The great conversation*. Chicago: Encyclopedia Britannica.

Larrabee, H. 1945. *Reliable knowledge*. Boston: Houghton Mifflin.

Lipman, M. et al. 1980. *Philosophy in the classroom*. 2nd ed. Philadelphia: Temple University Press.

Phenix, P. 1964. *Realms of meaning*, 233–64. New York: McGraw-Hill.

Ward, V. 1980. *Differential education for the gifted*, 170–79. Los Angeles: National/State Leadership Training Institute on the Gifted and the Talented.

EMPIRICS

Descriptive Treatment for Empirics

The process that stresses factual descriptions, generalizations, theoretical formulations, and explanations based on observation and experimentation in the realms of matter, life, mind, and society. DEG emphasizes the empirical method because of the extensive intellectual capacities of gifted learners.

Prescriptive Treatment for Empirics

DEG should provide generative and graded scientific experiences involving abstractions, classifications, generalizations, and complex formulations. DEG should focus on functional relationships among all types of knowledge that lead to the sequential development of scientific knowledge about knowledge.

Discussion on Empirics

Scientific inquiry through DEG brings order and intelligibility to information that originally presented itself in a miscellaneous and random profusion of claimed fact. Scientific inquiry in DEG helps the gifted learner to classify relevant and irrelevant data in the formulation of hypotheses which later must be confirmed or refuted.

In DEG, the scope of empirics should encompass the DEG core and a wide range of electives. Both curricular divisions demand a rigorous application of scientific method. The outcome must lead to an understanding of science as an objective and systematic means to probe for truth or falsehood. Knowledge production (KP) in empirics implies the ability to go beyond the current body of accepted scientific "facts."

The DEG educationists must introduce "generic concepts" and "great ideas" essential to the realm of empirics. Generic concepts that should be understood and utilized by all gifted learners include data, hypothesis, measurement, method, and taxonomy. Great ideas with which the gifted learner should wrestle are cause and effect, confirmation and refutation, creation and evolution, form and matter, objectivity and subjectivity, and truth and falsehood.

See Also

Discovery approach; observation; problem approach.

Related Concepts

Confirmation; epistemology; knowledge; objectivity; -ologies and -isms; order; refutation; science; testing; "Wissenschaft."

Suggested Readings

Cassidy, H. 1969. *Knowledge, experience and action*. New York: Columbia Teachers College Press.

Phenix, P. 1964. *Realms of meaning*. New York: McGraw-Hill.

Reid, L. 1961. *Ways of knowledge and experience*. New York: Oxford University Press.

Ward, V. 1980. *Differential education for the gifted*. Los Angeles: National/State Leadership Training Institute on the Gifted and the Talented.

ESTHETICS

Descriptive Treatment for Esthetics

The branch of philosophy dealing with the beautiful as a quality either in an object or an experience. As such, it involves the gifted learner in the various applied arts: music, the visual arts, the art of movement, and literature.

Prescriptive Treatment for Esthetics

DEG should recognize esthetics as that realm of meaning which offers the fullest expression of the gifted learner's creative potential and should extend the learner's ability to the recognition, analysis, and evaluation of beauty in all forms of artistic expression.

Discussion on Esthetics

The gifted learner and the DEG educationist should understand the importance of applied esthetics as a means to unleash creativity. Both need to understand artistic expression in historical context and in a variety of forms. Furthermore, the gifted learner and the educationist should engage in the study of art and its relation to the other realms of meaning, particularly symbolics, synnoetics, and synoptics. Both should consider art from the numerous theoretical and critical viewpoints concerning beauty. In the area of esthetic theory, knowledge production (KP) consists of expanding or elucidating knowledge beyond what is currently known. In terms of esthetic application, knowledge production comprises the creation of art objects and artistic expressions that go beyond conventional approaches.

The DEG educationist must introduce certain "generic concepts" and "great ideas" essential to the realm of esthetics. Generic concepts that should be known and understood by all gifted learners include creativity, emotion, great art, great dance, great literature, great music, imagination, sign and symbol. Great ideas with which the gifted learner must grapple are those of beauty, esthetic form and function, and esthetic judgment.

See Also

Differentiation; interest approach; observation.

Related Concepts

Color; critique; expressiveness; intuition; mood; perception; receptivity.

Suggested Readings

Osborn, W., and B. Rohan. 1931. *Enriching the curriculum for gifted children*. New York: The Macmillan Company.

Phenix, P. 1964. *Realms of meaning*, 139–85. New York: McGraw-Hill.

Swift, E. 1908. *Mind in the making*. New York: Charles Scribner's Sons.

Ward, V. 1980. *Differential education for the gifted*. Los Angeles: National/State Leadership Training Institute on the Gifted and the Talented.

SYMBOLICS

Descriptive Treatment for Symbolics

The study of language/linguistics, mathematics/logic, and such nondiscursive forms as gestures, rituals, and patterns. Symbolic structures contain meanings with socially understood formation and transformation rules created as instruments for expression, information, and communication. The gifted have the potential to become masters of these rules in order to achieve a high degree of symbolic literacy.

Prescriptive Treatment for Symbolics

DEG should engage the imagination of the gifted learner through interpretation of and elaboration on diverse expressions of meanings and trigger interest and motivation in the gifted learner to explore new symbolic codes. DEG should focus on symbolics as a means to express an infinite variety of experiences that represent the real world in all of its depth and complexity.

Discussion on Symbolics

Symbolic systems in DEG are fundamental to the expression of meaning in all content areas. Symbolics in DEG helps the gifted learner to analyze, utilize, criticize, master, and elaborate on symbolic forms and codes.

In DEG, symbolics should experiment with all symbolic forms in the DEG core as well as the electives. H_2O, for example, is a symbolic expression for water; however, the symbolic meaning of water must go beyond this concrete chemical reference. Both curricular divisions demand symbolic diversity for reflective understanding to occur. The outcome must lead to an understanding of the use of various symbols to economize time and materials. Knowledge production (KP) in symbolics implies the ability to participate in the creation of new symbolic forms, unusual expressions, and novel abstractions.

In symbolics, the DEG educationist must introduce the gifted learner to such "generic concepts" as axioms, codes, concepts, constructs, expressions, forms, formulas, fragments, gestures, paradigms, rhythms, rituals, signs, structures, syllogisms, symbols, systems, and theorems. "Great ideas" with which the gifted learner should wrestle are abstraction, artificiality, generalization, mearning, naturalness, spontaneity, and theory.

See Also

Games/play approach; observation; systems approach.

Related Concepts

Ideation; insight; semiotic function.

Suggested Readings

Guilford, J. P. 1950. "Creativity." *The American Psychologist* 5:444–54.

Forty ninth yearbook of the National Society for the Study of Education. Part 1. 1950. Chicago: University of Chicago Press.

DISCOVERY APPROACH

Descriptive Treatment for Discovery Approach

The process of learning principles and concepts which occurs as a generalization of experiences on the part of the gifted learner in the absence of direct tellings by the instructor or others. Discovery learning is an important instructional procedure in DEG to be applied to all content areas for knowledge production to take place.

Prescriptive Treatment for Discovery Approach

In DEG, certain information and generalizations must be withheld in order to encourage exploration and experimentation necessary for the gifted learner to "discover" the rule, concept, principle, or generalization. This method reinforces the kind of inferential thinking imperative for new discoveries to be made in all realms of knowledge.

Discussion on Discovery Approach

The discovery approach is liable to gross misinterpretation in many DEG learning situations. To advocate such an approach as a learning method without the prior attainment and recall of certain empirical rules (for example, scientific method) makes no sense (Gagné, 1977, pp. 164–65). DEG sees a necessity for the teaching of empirical rules prior to problem solving and discovery learning. Such rules deal with the collection and classification of data, the interpretation of data, and the formulation as well as the testing of hypotheses. After the mastery of these fundamental rules, transfer can take place to a problem involving new ideas, new rules, or new methods.

DEG also asserts that the discovery of scientific phenomena cannot and should not be separated from social aspects. DEG's "Science and Society Program" (SSP) is based on the British Nuffield schemes and Dutch Leiden projects, which provide ample opportunity for empirical inquiry, pupil participation in experimentation, and weighing of consequences on social grounds. Focusing on social issues, paralleled by scientific investigations, leads to discussions that address technical, economic, and political problems. The general aims of SSP are: to stimulate gifted students to think about relevant scientific issues; to collect additional materials in order to back a choice or an argument; to consult outside experts; and to discuss or share findings with peers, the regular schools, and/or the community at large. An additional effort is made to produce publishable term papers that address the scientific issue within its social context.

Finally, in regard to discovery learning, Leiden's "Physics and Society Program" (PSP) in Dutch schools lists three aims.

1. To discover how physics is part of the world and the culture in which we live.
2. To gain insight in our own position and possibilities in the world of physics.
3. To acquire subject literacy; that is, to become a mature, reflective, and alert citizen who is able to form a considered judgment on important policy issues and, thus, enabling him or her to participate in procedural democracy (adapted from Rip, 1980, p. 6).

See Also

Differentiation; enrichment.

Related Concepts

Heuristic learning; inductive learning; inquiry learning; laboratory method; problem method.

Suggested Readings

Gagné, R. 1977. *The conditions of learning*, 3rd ed., 155–79. New York: Holt.

Holton, G. 1978. *The scientific imagination*. London: Cambridge University Press.

Rip, A. 1980. *Science and society education in Dutch schools*. Paper presented at the University of London Institute of Education, London.

GAMES/PLAY APPROACH

Descriptive Treatment for Games/Play Approach

In DEG, play is seen as a voluntary activity pursued without ulterior purpose and, on the whole, with enjoyment or expectation of enjoyment (even though certain elements of play may not be enjoyed); game is utilized as a form of organized play with a set of definite rules and different roles for participants to play in a competitive setting. DEG uses play *and* games as means "to learn how to enjoy learning."

Prescriptive Treatment for Games/Play Approach

Play is utilized in DEG because it adds spontaneity, non-restrictiveness, imagination, and fun to the learning process. Games are prescribed because they require an appropriate mixture of chance and skill. They reinforce initiative, risk taking, competition, and purpose. Both approaches allow for cooperation, competition, and originality—elements which are seen as pedagogical essentials for DEG in order to create an achievement-oriented and enjoyable learning climate.

Discussion on Games/Play Approach

The games/play approach in DEG serves as a pedagogical technique and a constructive outlet for the gifted learner's high sense of humor, spontaneity, enjoyment in learning, and intellectual rigor. The relationships between play, imagination, game, and playfulness and their dependence on humor, spontaneity, and joy are illustrated in Figure 1 (partially adapted from Lieberman, 1977, p. 108).

DEG also reinforces the "producer approach" to humor by constructively building connections between student interest and productive thinking. Student-designed games and plays are

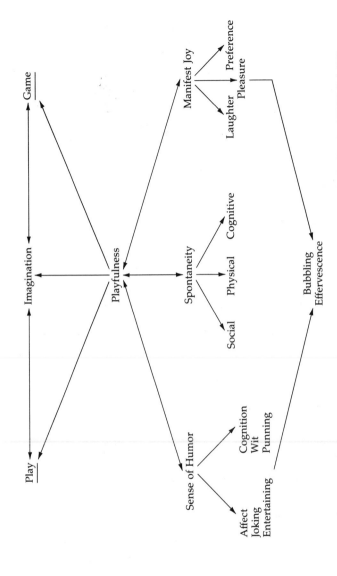

RELATIONSHIPS AMONG ELEMENTS IN THE GAMES/PLAY APPROACH

means to relearn or to restructure the learning environment for the emergence of a more open, tolerant, and playful style in dealing with new situations, problems, or events. But a healthy balance between joy derived from competition (for example, tournaments) and cooperation (for instance, simulations) is of paramount importance. It is always necessary that DEG educationists ask themselves whether the enjoyment derives from plays or games that emphasize the positive or the negative (that is, the friendly or the hostile) ingredients of intrinsic motivation (Lieberman, 1977, pp. 72–80).

This approach to enjoy learning has the following intrinsic values:

1. The attention-focusing quality on part of the learner is high.
2. The active student involvement is based on student-initiated and student-executed games/play situations that incorporate competition, fairness, and cooperation. These ingredients should produce enjoyment for all.
3. The diminishing effect of teacher authority is based on a change of roles (for example, judge or jury) and not on the outcome of the play or game (that is, winning or losing) (Bruner et al., 1976, p. 462).

See Also

Imagination; interest; interest approach; motivation.

Related Concepts

Academic games; gaming; playfulness; play therapy; role-playing; simulation(s); social education.

Suggested Readings

Bruner, J. et al. eds. 1976. *Play: Its role in development and evolution*, 461–63. Harmondsworth, England: Penguin.
Lieberman, J. 1977. *Playfulness*, 72–80. New York: Academic Press.

INTEREST APPROACH

Descriptive Treatment for Interest Approach

The pedagogical process that utilizes the wide range of interests of the gifted learner in determining both the content and the methods of instruction. DEG applies this approach because of its motivational nature.

Prescriptive Treatment for Interest Approach

Entrusting gifted learners with curiosity, drive, and responsibility for lifelong learning results in greater academic, personal, and social achievements. Gifted learners should be able to assess their interests and be allowed to plan and execute a self-initiated curriculum in which they move from little or no knowledge of a self-chosen topic to a level of excellence in form of student projects or products. Evocation of gifted learner's interests, therefore, is critical to DEG.

Discussion on Interest Approach

The interest approach sets out to formulate a pedagogical strategy that helps DEG educationists capitalize on the gifted learner's wide range of interests and high level of motivation.

This technique has the following objectives:

1. To integrate cognitive, affective, conative, and psychomotoric learning (Bruner's notion of confluent education [1960]).
2. To implement nondirected inquiry teaching (discovery learning).
3. To strengthen team work and cooperation among gifted students (procedural democracy).
4. To augment democratic decision making (leadership training).

5. To allow for interaction between DEG staff, gifted students, and community resources (sharing of generative knowledge and know-how).
6. To permit gifted students to initiate, to plan, and to execute a student-centered curriculum ("educere" pedagogy).
7. To entrust gifted learners with a responsibility for learning as an ongoing process (life-time education).
8. To show that commitment and persistence can lead to excellence and perfection as aspiring values of human endeavor (Magoon and Jellen, 1980, p. 4).

Magoon and Jellen's (1980) "SIU O-100 Approach" incorporates these objectives and encourages the gifted to move from little or no knowledge (O) concerning a given interest area (SIU or Student Interest Unit) to a level of excellence (100). This learning model is based on "educere" principles (that is, the leading out of gifted potentialities) and provides a sequential approach to programmatic enrichment, addressing "learning how to learn and share" as a major proposition for DEG.

See Also

Discovery approach; enrichment; interest; motivation; problem approach.

Related Concepts

Activity curriculum; self-activity; self-education; self-motivation; Student Interest Unit (SIU); SIU O-100 Approach.

Suggested Readings

Bruner, J. 1960. *The process of education*. Cambridge, MA: Harvard University Press.

Magoon, R., and H. Jellen. 1980. *Educational strategies—the SIU 0-100: Capitalizing on student interests and motivation*. Poquoson, VA: Human Development Press.

Renzulli, J. 1980. *The interest-a-lyzer*. Mansfield, CT: Creative Learning Press.

POLYTECHNICAL APPROACH

Descriptive Treatment for Polytechnical Approach

The process that focuses on the applied sciences and arts by stressing a variety of technical studies and skills necessary for knowledge production to occur. DEG stresses the polytechnical approach to encourage gifted learners to understand their distinctive role in society as knowledge producers.

Prescriptive Treatment for Polytechnical Approach

DEG must introduce gifted learners to the major forces of economy and industry on a comparative basis. This approach is an attempt to apply theory to practice through simulations, hobby circles, competitive projects, and/or mentorships.

Discussion on Polytechnical Approach

The polytechnical approach or principle can easily be transferred to the democratic context, even though it is frequently associated with the Soviet system of education (polytechnicalism). The objectives of this approach are, nevertheless, worth considering for DEG.

Polytechnical education in the context of this discussion has the task of developing each individual to the full extent of his or her abilities so that he or she might accept his or her responsibilities as a productive citizen and promote the growth of a progressive democratic society. Fundamental to the achievement of this DEG aim is the acquisition of correct attitudes towards work, of a knowledge of production methods, and of technical skills based upon theoretical principles (Holmes, 1961). In reality, then, DEG has to be linked with productive labor or with socially useful work such as community projects or voluntary assistance programs.

Other important tenets include the abolishment of the deforming divorce between mental and manual work and an attempt to bridge the gap between DEG programs, normal schooling, and vocational training. The polytechnical approach becomes, therefore, a means to share knowledge and know-how with others in order to allow for maximum interaction between gifted students and the community at large. Professional apprenticeship programs (Virginia Beach Public Schools, Virginia) or occupational mentorships (Phoenix Public Schools, Arizona) are supported by evidence showing increased cooperation and motivation in learning situations when gifted students have an opportunity to work directly under the guidance of model professionals and model community leaders. Similar tutorial relationships can be established on a contractual basis between gifted students, their teachers, and fellow pupils. These are important educational considerations for democratic leadership to emerge and to guard against elitist stratification, insulation, or isolation of gifted youth.

See Also

Leadership

Related Concepts

Industrial processes/techniques; industrial skills; labor processes; liberal/modern education; mentorship; performance studies; production methods; project method; technological studies; vocational training; work ethics; working conditions.

Suggested Readings

Holmes, B. 1961. Polytechnical education in the U.S.S.R. Reprinted in *Bulletin of the Institute of Physics* (University of London), 58–62.

Shapovalenko, S., ed., 1963. *Polytechnical education in the U.S.S.R.* Amsterdam, Holland: UNESCO.

PROBLEM APPROACH

Descriptive Treatment for Problem Approach

The process of instruction by which learning is stimulated through the creation of challenging situations that demand solution or by which perplexing questions can be brought to a satisfactory resolution formulated by the gifted. DEG affords problems to gifted learners in order to challenge them academically, personally, and/or socially.

Prescriptive Treatment for Problem Approach

DEG must assist the gifted learner with the application of previously learned rules to achieve possible solutions for novel situations. Educationists must arrange for relevant learning conditions so that transfer to an entirely different domain of problems can be made (for example, generalization and transfer of "academic problems" to personal, social, environmental, and/or institutional conditions).

Discussion on Problem Approach

Although there are different kinds of problems and different kinds of abilities involved in the solving of a problem, there is a generic pattern of events to which the solution of a problem conforms (Guilford, 1968). Guilford lists models that have been proposed by various authors concerning problem solving, creative production, and invention, as indicated in Table 6.

See Also

Imagination; intelligence.

Related Concepts

Cognitive strategy(ies); colligation; deduction; enquiry; generalizability; heuristic method; hypothetico-deductive

Table 6. Steps in the Solution of a Problem in Productive Thinking as Seen by Dewey (1910), Wallas (1945), Rossman (1931), and Holmes (1973): Similarities and Differences [1]

Dewey	Wallas	Rossman	Holmes
Difficulty felt		Need or difficulty observed	State of confusion: desire to think
Difficulty located and defined		Problem formulated	Intellectualization of the problem
	Preparation (information gathered)	Available information surveyed	Identification of asynchronous change in environmental, institutional, and normative terms
	Incubation (unconscious work going on)		
Possible solutions suggested	Illumination (solutions emerge)	Solutions formulated	Formulation of hypothesis (tentative solutions)
Consequences	Verification (solutions tested and elaborated)	Solutions critically examined	Hypothesis and emerging alternative solutions empirically tested
		New ideas formulated	
Solution is accepted		New ideas tested and accepted	Implementation and evaluation of policy

1. Partially adopted from Guilford, 1968, p. 201

method; induction; inference(s); KP, or knowledge production; pragmatism; problem solving; productive thinking; rule learning; transfer; utilitarianism.

Suggested Readings

Guilford, J. 1968. *Intelligence, creativity, and educational implications*. San Diego: Knapp.

SYSTEMS APPROACH

Descriptive Treatment for Systems Approach

The process whereby the parameters or boundaries of a structure of an organized whole are established and the actual or possible inputs and outputs to the structure are identified and critically examined. DEG helps gifted learners define the boundaries of a given system and review what is required to improve or enhance that system.

Prescriptive Treatment for Systems Approach

General systems theory is an important but often neglected area of study in DEG. The ability of gifted learners to construct systems is a characteristic of complex, productive, and innovative thinking. The analysis, understanding, and production of systemic models are recommended as truly differential contents particularly suited for the gifted in the light of knowledge production.

Discussion on Systems Approach

Guilford (1968) states:

"One of the most neglected processes in present creative-training procedures and yet one of the most important of the common creative processes found in the very productive creator, is the construction of systems. Most descriptions of what creative persons do mention is that relatively early in the total sequence of events some kind of system appears, whether it be a theme, a story plot, a motif, or some other kind of outline affair. This is the backbone, the skeleton, or framework of the major production to come. Within the total framework, subsystems are also developed, such as melodies and phrases in music, stanzas in poems, equations in a mathematical development, and part devices within major inventions" (p. 212).

The chief implication of Guilford's statements for DEG is that DEG educationists must pay attention to systems building. Content per se does not really matter initially, and the composition may change several times, but the very notion of outlining, arranging, and rearranging the proposed whole or "Gestalt" is seen as an essential part in the development of cognitive schema of potential knowledge producers. In terms of fluency of ideational production by way of transfer, information that deals by its very nature with systems and classes seems particularly appropriate (Guilford, 1967, p. 345).

The systems approach in DEG tries to accomplish systems analysis, systems design, and systems evaluation by focusing on those systemic criteria that affect the gifted student's personal, social, and academic life. Taxonomies, hierarchies, organizations, and cultural codes are good places to start studying systems as a major facet of qualitatively differential DEG contents.

The identification and analysis of ideal-seeking systems seem to be especially appropriate for those who have the capacities for knowledge production. This systemic move from descriptive systems to prescriptive ones is still in its infancy. DEG, especially, has the potential to advance systems theory along these lines. Unlimited progress can be made on any of the four ideal-seeking fronts: (1) the ideal politico-economic system providing plenty for all; (2) the ideal scientific system of truth; (3) the ideal ethico-moral system of good; and (4) the ideal aesthetic system of beauty (Ackoff and Emery, 1972, p. 246). Gifted individuals seem to be ideally suited for this kind of systemic study.

See Also

Discovery approach; imagination; intelligence; leadership; polytechnical approach; problem approach.

Related Concepts

Communication and information theory(ies); cybernetics (organism and mechanism); general systems theory; interactionism; organization per se; synthetic approach; taxonomy; teleology; transmission theory.

Suggested Readings

Ackoff, R., and F. Emery. 1972. *On purposeful systems*. London: Tavistock.

Guilford, J. 1967. *The nature of human intelligence*, 312–45. New York: McGraw-Hill.

———. 1968. *Intelligence, creativity, and their educational implications*, 196–213. San Diego: Knapp.

ACHIEVEMENT

Descriptive Treatment for Achievement

The process used to describe accomplishment or proficiency in performance in all content areas chosen for DEG. This total performance can be measured by a series of standardized tests, auditions, and/or student projects.

Prescriptive Treatment for Achievement

Achievement is a matter of attitude and adjustment. Gifted learners differ with respect to their willingness or unwillingness to deal with the demands or sameness of normal schooling. Low-gifted achievers are less well-adjusted, more aggressive, bored with schooling, and have low occupational aspirations. Their high-achieving peers show opposite tendencies. DEG educationists must provide an "environmental challenge" with expectancy and attractiveness of success in all gifted learners.

Discussion on Achievement

Achievement clearly depends on the instruction and training given as well as on the gifted person's attitude, aptitude, motivation, and interest. Thus, both personality and environmental factors must be considered in accounting for the strength of motivation to achieve. Most types of school achievement can be assessed by objective measures (for example, standardized scholastic achievement tests). Some types of achievement, however, are more complex (for instance, artistic creations) or more qualitative than quantitative, and must be evaluated by the judgment of experts (Vernon et al., 1977).

Gifted students differ greatly in their motive to achieve and to succeed. Key factors for success in school and life are family background, test scores in school, years of schooling completed, and personality characteristics such as perseverance and prudence (Jencks, 1979). It is, therefore, the task of the DEG educationist to introduce the gifted learner to the dynamics of achievement-oriented behavior by providing him with a challenging environment that reinforces competitive and gamelike situations with high risk factors. An achievement-oriented climate in a classroom setting of gifted learners should incorporate the following (Covington and Beery, 1976, pp. 126–41):

—setting standards of excellence
—taking risks
—participating in competitive games
—recognizing the relationship between realistic goal setting and success
—engaging in self-evaluations
—allowing for responsibility
—providing for independent work
—insisting upon task analysis and task completion.

But it also must be recognized that even gifted students in a challenging environment are unequal in their capacities and attainments. The notion of equality of opportunity recognizes, however, the differences of endowment and motivation and accepts the certainty of differences in achievement. Allowing free play to these differences and freedom to excel accounts for much in terms of individual excellence and aspiration. Both are crucial elements in any achieving society with high expectations and a competitive edge.

See Also

Evaluation; games/play approach; interest; motivation.

Related Concepts

Achievement motive; adjustment; aspiration; attitude; desire; drive; effort; forethought; motivation; need, perseverance; prudence; risk; self-confidence; success; task; will.

Suggested Readings

Covington, M., and R. Beery. 1976. *Self-worth and school learning*, 126–41. New York: Holt, Rinehart & Winston.
Jencks, C. 1980. *Who gets ahead?* New York: Basic Books.

EVALUATION

Descriptive Treatment for Evaluation

The process of assessing the success of a course of study, set of learning experiences, or a particular curriculum development during (formative) and after their implementation and termination (summative). Evaluation in DEG emphasizes assessment for gifted learners in an achievement-oriented climate as well as assessment of educationists and the community.

Prescriptive Treatment for Evaluation

Formal and informal assessment procedures must be designed and implemented to ascertain the achievement of gifted learners during and after learning experiences. Furthermore, the Diagnostic and Evaluative Scales for Differential Education of the Gifted (DESDEG) are designed and prescribed for two reasons: first, institutional self-study—individuals and committees who are in charge of local DEG reflect upon the nature of their efforts, and second, professional evaluation—a formalized sequence of descriptive/prescriptive reports for the purposes of observation and inquiry toward the development and improvement of a given DEG program.

Discussion on Evaluation

The instrument used for program evaluation (see Appendix B) is partially adapted from Renzulli and Ward (1969). Four theoretical distinctions focus on a minimal number of key features: student, educator, knowledge, and society. All four distinctions can be linked with some realizable aim or end. They make the greatest contribution to educational theory as guidelines for the purpose of prescribing and recommending what is to be understood and to be done in formative and summative evaluation procedures. They help DEG educationists realize those educational ends that depend ultimately on considerations of value: the value of the gifted learner, the value of the educationist, the value of generative knowledge, and the value of knowledge production and leadership training in a democratic society.

Successful evaluation should be conducted by trained DEG personnel *not* affiliated with a given DEG program. The outcome should trigger

    — improved identification and placement programs
    — improved methods of instruction
    — improved instructional materials
    — desired behavioral changes
    — generative knowledge offerings that meet the demands of a changing society and the need of knowledge producers (partially adapted from Ward et al., 1962, p. 79).

Twelve general program requirements (*four* key features: student, educator, knowledge, and society at *three* different levels: normative, tactical, and strategic) are consistent with DEG theory and educational decision making. On the normative level (policy formulation), the validity of the concept behind each key feature must be communicated to all decision-making levels directly or indirectly involved in a DEG program. On the tactical level (policy implementation), policy must address and assess the roles and responsibilities of the entire DEG staff. This level also provides guidelines for program organization and allocation of resources. On the strategic level (program operation), the instrument assesses relationships between generative knowledge and the overall objectives of DEG. It also acknowledges public-relations work concerning attitudinal changes toward the acceptance of DEG programs in a given community. The corresponding specific program requisites are self-explanatory and are followed by a practical rating scale (+1; 0; or −1).

See Also

Achievement; Appendix B; mental testing; observation.

Related Concepts

Course evaluation; DESDEG; Diagnostic and Evaluative Scales for Differential Education for the Gifted; program evaluation; success.

Suggested Readings

Jellen, H. 1981. Programme evaluation in differential education for the gifted (DEG). *New Horizons in Education: The Journal of the World Education Fellowship in Australia* 65:26–32.

Renzulli, J., and V. Ward. 1969. *Diagnostic and evaluative scales for differential education of the gifted (DESDEG).* Charlottesville, VA: University of Virginia. (Copies may be obtained from the authors).

Ward, V. et al. 1962. *The gifted student: A manual for program improvement.* Atlanta: Southern Regional Education Board, 79.

OBSERVATION

Descriptive Treatment for Observation

The methodology of gathering information on gifted learners by viewing their total behavior in a variety of situations. DEG does this by using such naturalistic observation devices as one-way screens, observation domes, time samplings, interviews, interaction process analyses, diary or log descriptions, trait ratings, and field unit analyses.

Prescriptive Treatment for Observation

DEG requires the study of gifted behavior directly in naturalistic settings (for example, during play and games sessions, independent study, and group interaction) to get an accurate assessment of the gifted learner's total behavior. Through direct observation of gifted learners a personal profile can be developed that corresponds closely to the concepts of characterology and personalysis. The results of such data gathering and data analyses of gifted behavior(s) must contribute to an advancement of DEG theory and practice.

Discussion on Observation Techniques

DEG relies, along with the application of mental tests, on observation techniques to select educators and gifted students for DEG programs and to evaluate their performance or behaviorism. Since there is a multitude of ethological or naturalistic methods, only the more relevant ones have been selected for treatment in this discussion:

Biography can be an excellent source of direct or indirect observation and understanding. The observers apply this interpretative method not only to sift and select facts, but also to understand the personality behind the written material. This kind of study is recommended as a prelude to the involvement of gifted learners in the writing of autobiographies, diaries, and personal logs.

Autobiographies and *diaries* differ in one essential aspect: the latter concentrate on an assessment of acts and events of the present, while autobiographies also include the past by giving additional attention to attitudes and interpretative thoughts. Both provide important clues for a personalysis of the writer.

Dream journals can be especially helpful when they deal with descriptions of friends, enemies, threats, relatives, and acquaintances. This subconscious form of self-observation can be particularly helpful for psychological support personnel that might have to be consulted for therapeutic-corrective intervention.

Questionnaires and *inventories* apply to introspective criteria and usually address questions such as "What will you do if confronted with such and such an event?" These questions frame the expected answers, revealing past, present, and future experiences of the gifted individual.

Psychognosis refers to character sketches written by the learner after the viewing of a provocative film or the reading of a controversial novel. Role playing and videotaping of such character sketches unfold an incredible amount of personalytic data.

Videotaping of student-teacher interactions, play sessions, independent work, and free time leads to valuable findings dealing with cognitive, affective, conative, and psychomotoric behaviors that can later be recorded into personalysis charts kept for research purposes on DEG educationists and learners (partially adapted from Roback, 1952, pp. 548–61).

All of these observations or naturalistic methods need community approval. Workshops for parents and teachers must reveal the importance of these techniques for the assessment and understanding of gifted behavior on the whole.

See Also

Characterology; evaluation; interest approach; mental testing.

Related Concepts

Audio-visual recordings; checklist(s); data collecting; descriptions (molecular and molar categories); ethnogram building; ethology; event recording; interview(s); observational study(ies)—direct/indirect and naturalistic/non-naturalistic; questionnaire(s); schema or set of criteria.

Suggested Readings

Blurton-Jones, N. 1972. *Ethological studies of child behavior*. Cambridge, England: Cambridge Univ. Press.

Roback, A. 1952. *The psychology of character*. 3rd ed. London: Routledge and Kegan.

THE NEEDS OF SOCIETY
KEY CONCEPTS

A.1   Democracy
A.2   Equality
B.1   Responsibility
B.2   Responsiveness

DEMOCRACY

Descriptive Treatment for Democracy

The form of government or decision-making process in which the supreme power is retained by the people and the "ruled" are able to accept or reject authority. DEG encourages democratic procedure as a method of participation by all gifted learners in order to prepare them for life in a democratic society.

Prescriptive Treatment for Democracy

The DEG educationist should realize that socialization of the gifted learner in a democratic society can be achieved best through practice of the democratic ideal. Full and equal participation by all gifted individuals in the solution of relevant problems of common concern encourages social equality and honors differences among individuals and their ideas.

Discussion on Democracy

In DEG, the functioning ideal by which the school operates must be clear. Since the functioning ideal of the school should be the same as that of the society for which the gifted learner is being socialized, the functioning ideal of the school in a democracy should be the democratic ideal. Since the DEG educationist's practice should aid in fostering the desired ideal(s), he or she must conduct classes democratically, which means that the gifted learners must share the power to shape the classroom environment by consensus. Such a democratic classroom environment, if consistent with society, will socialize the gifted learner in terms of both leadership training and submission to the consensus of the majority. Because in society the gifted learner will not necessarily be part of an elite governing body answerable only to itself, the gifted must spend time in regular classrooms as well.

Here they will learn to accept the necessity of sharing authority and knowledge with intellectually less gifted students, as well as with other classroom teachers.

See Also

Equality; ethics; leadership training.

Related Concepts

Centralization; citizenship; decentralization; federalism; montesquieuism; pragmatism; utilitarianism.

Suggested Readings

Adler, M. 1982. *The paideia proposal*, 3–8. New York: Macmillan.
Cubberley, E. 1919. *Public education in the United States*, 111–15, 479–80. Boston: Houghton Mifflin.
Dewey, J. 1916. *Democracy and education*. New York: Macmillan.
Ward, V. 1980. *Differential education for the gifted*, 181–220. Los Angeles: National/State Leadership Training Institute on the Gifted and Talented.

EQUALITY

Descriptive Treatment for Equality

The ideal of providing all humans with similar opportunity and treatment on the basis of their common humanity. DEG encourages social and political equality and rejects elitist snobbery among and between gifted learners as well as others.

Prescriptive Treatment for Equality

The DEG educationist should provide equal but differentiated educational opportunities for all gifted learners. DEG should be characterized by justice, fairness, and equal treatment of all participants.

Discussion on Equality

In DEG, the ideal of equality must be approached through both theory and practice. While, in accord with the democratic ideal, all human beings should be given equal treatment and equal opportunity as human beings on the basis of their common humanity, differential treatment is both permissible and desirable on the basis of individual mental differences. First, all students should be given the opportunity to be identified as either gifted or nongifted. Second, once giftedness has been identified, differential educational treatment of the gifted is desirable in order to enhance their personal, social, and academic growth; similarly, those on the opposite side of the mental scale may have received differential treatment for years without being labeled "elitist." Neither the gifted nor the nongifted are guaranteed fulfillment of their educational aspirations. DEG, however, is firmly based on the Jeffersonian ideal of democracy and equality, which requires equal educational opportunity for all to progress according to talent and merit. This Jeffersonian interpretation of egalitarianism rests on the faith that the welfare of the Republic depends on educated citizens, who need to be counseled, not necessarily led, by the most capable—the gifted.

See Also

Acceleration; achievement; democracy; differentiation; ethics.

Related Concepts

Democracy; egalitarianism.

Suggested Readings

Adler, M. 1982. *The paideia proposal*, 15–36. New York: Macmillan.

Butts, R. 1955. *A cultural history of western education*, 435–43. New York: McGraw-Hill.

Jones, L. 1980. *Great expectations*, 149–65. New York: Ballantine.

Ward, V. 1980. *Differential education for the gifted*, 181–220. Los Angeles: National/State Leadership Training Institute on the Gifted and Talented.

RESPONSIBILITY

Descriptive Treatment for Responsibility

The quality or state of being accountable and/or liable for one's conduct and obligations in relationship to others. This quality addresses leadership and the application of such generalized moral principles as equality, fairness, liberty, and respect for others.

Prescriptive Treatment for Responsibility

DEG should help the gifted learner consider each act in a consequential relationship to other acts. DEG should encourage each learner to weigh consequences by establishing a personally reasoned connection between questionable knowledge and social responsibility. Since procedural democracy is in need of responsible knowledge producers to serve as leaders, DEG should become the training ground for responsible, social, as well as academic leadership.

Discussion on Responsibility

Through experiences in the educational design of the DEG core and electives, the gifted learner must accept the role of responsible world stewardship. In DEG, the potential for gifted learners to become effective leaders will be fulfilled when the gifted learner formulates a strategy to actualize ideal leadership qualities. Instruction must concentrate on fundamental human motives and on the less-than-ideal behavior patterns that have evolved in a social context to satisfy these motives.

The DEG educationist must provide the gifted learner with a general knowledge of philosophy, a more specific knowledge of ethics, and a facility to recognize and clarify the consequences caused by human actions. Furthermore, the educationist must provide opportunities for public debate and discussion in which the gifted learners voice their concerns on current issues and/or problems that will affect their lives or the lives of others. "The Mentor Academy Program (MAP)," for example, is a skill-based model for training gifted high-school students as mentors. "Through a series of training sessions, students learn skill assessment, acquisition, application, apprenticeship, and anticipation in order to work more effectively with mentors, and to become mentors for others in the community as well as for themselves. This training not only realizes and recognizes the potential of the gifted to use community resources more effectively but also to serve the needs of the community and themselves better. It gives students the knowledge of new technologies to cope and to create within an information society" (Runions, p. 1).

See Also

Ethics; leadership training; responsiveness; restructuring; sensitivity.

Related Concepts

Accountability; altruism; civic development; cooperation; humanistic education; mentorship; stewardship.

Suggested Readings

Jellen, H. 1985. The meaning and justification for DEG in a democracy: A taxonomical approach. In *Gifted Education International* 3(2):14–20.

Runions, R. 1982. *Stewardship: Training the gifted as community mentors* (Contract No. 400-81-0031). Washington: National Institute of Education.

RESPONSIVENESS

Descriptive Treatment for Responsiveness

The quality of being ready or inclined to react to and assist others through cooperative social activity. The degree to which the gifted social leader can use his or her superior abilities in action depends on the skill of responding to the needs of all human beings and the motivational level of the gifted.

Prescriptive Treatment for Responsiveness

DEG can enhance responsiveness by analyzing the origin and function of such behavioral dynamics as attitudes, beliefs, emotions, misconceptions, motives, perceptions, prejudices, and values. DEG should help the gifted learner develop cooperation through critical thinking since cooperation is an essential and civic function in a procedural democracy. DEG experiences should engage the gifted learner in communal work to develop the ability to act as a problem solver in the community. All societies are in need of responsive knowledge producers to serve as change agents.

Discussion on Responsiveness

The gifted learner is particularly fit to deal with change and rapid developments. The DEG core and electives should help the gifted learner to realize the significance of change and, therefore, to foresee, anticipate, cope with, and adapt to change. The explosion of knowledge, population, and public expectations will create sensitive academic, social, political, and economic fronts that require responsive action from those who have the capabilities to solve problems. DEG is a response to problems that affect American society and humanity at large. DEG becomes a real possibility for responding to such old problems as disease, injustice, oppression, poverty, and war with new and fresh solutions.

It is the responsibility of the DEG educationist to point out those academic, social, and personal inadequacies that need improvement for the betterment of society as well as humankind. Responsiveness in DEG implies taking action for the sake of progress by overcoming the potential difficulties often displayed by disillusioned gifted individuals (for example, social alienation, personal frustration, or planned retaliation).

See Also

Ethics; leadership training; responsibility.

Related Concepts

Anticipatory thought; compassion; empathy; ethics; misanthropy; philanthropy.

Suggested Readings

Dewey, J. 1913. *Interest and effort in education.* Boston: Houghton Mifflin.

Gavian, R., ed. 1958. *The social education of the academically talented* (curriculum series no. 10). Washington: National Council for the Social Studies (a department of the National Education Association).

Hollingworth, L. 1926. *Gifted children: Their nature and nurture.* New York: Macmillan.

Ward, V. 1980. *Differential education for the gifted,* 86–101, 108–17, and 183–222. Los Angeles: National/State Leadership Training Institute on the Gifted and Talented.

APPENDIXES
BIBLIOGRAPHY

Appendix A
CHARACTEROLOGY AND PERSONALYSIS FOR DEG

APPLICATION OF PERSONALYTICAL RECORDINGS

Personalyses for cognition, affect, and conation demand from the DEG educationist a systematic recording of those mental qualities that distinguish the gifted from the general populace. The back-up charts for cognition, affect, and conation offer valid psychometric instruments with subsequent conversion of scores to assist the educationist with the accurate recording of mental capabilities characteristic of gifted learners. The systematic, accurate, and longitudinal recording of these types of data will contribute to the kind of meaningful DEG research necessary for the emergence of a science of DEG in general and a DEG characterology in particular.

PERSONALYSIS: COGNITION

Student's Name _____ Year _____

	I INTELLIGENCE		II IMAGINATION	III MEMORY	IV HUMOR	V SOCIAL INTELLIGENCE
	g-factor High I.Q.	s-factors High Academic Achievement	Ideational Flow	High Retention	Wit	High Social Intelligence
10						
9						
8						
7	7+ as indicator of cognitive exceptionality					
6						
5						
4						
3						
2						
1						
0						
	Low I.Q.	Low Academic Achievement	Ideational Stagnation	Low Retention	Lack of Wit	Low Social Intelligence

PERSONALYSIS: AFFECT

Student's Name _____   Year _____

	I	II	III	
	EMPATHY	SENSITIVITY	TEMPERAMENT	
	High Degree of Empathy	High Degree of Sensitivity	High Percentage Of Positive Temperament Traits	
10				10
9				9
8				8
7	7+ as indicator of affective exceptionality			7
6				6
5				5
4				4
3				3
2				2
1				1
0				0
	Low Degree of Empathy	Low Degree of Sensitivity	Low Percentage of Positive Temperament Traits	

PERSONALYSIS: CONATION

Student's Name _____ Year _____

	I	II	III
	INTERESTS	MOTIVATION	CURIOSITY
	Strong Preference for Working with Ideas	Strong Initiative and Drive	High Degree of Curiosity
10			
9			
8			
7	7+ as indicator of cognitive exceptionality		
6			
5			
4			
3			
2			
1			
0			
	Weak Preference for Working with Ideas	Lack of Initiative and Drive	Low Degree of Curiosity

Back-up Chart for Cognition

Factors to be Considered:	Sample Instruments:	Conversion of Scores:
I. Intelligence		
a. The *g* factor	*Wechsler Adult Intelligence Scale* (WAIS-R):	
	Measurements:	209 is top score. 146 on the WAIS-R equals 7 on the Personalysis for Cognition. 7+ indicates high IQ.
	—Verbal Scale—information, digit span, vocabulary, arithmetic, comprehension, and similarities.	
	—Performance Scale— picture comprehension and arrangement, block design, object assembly, and digital symbols.	
b. The *s* factors	*Iowa Tests of Educational Development* (ITED):	
	Measurements:	707 is top score. 495 on the ITED equal 7 on the Personalysis for Cognition. 7+ indicates high academic achievement.
	—Basic social concepts.	
	—Natural science.	
	—Correctness and appropriateness of expression.	
	—Quantitative thinking.	
	—Social science.	
	—Literary materials.	
	—General vocabulary.	
	—Uses of sources of information.	

Back-up Chart for Cognition (*continued*)

Factors to be Considered:	Sample Instruments:	Conversion of Scores:
II. Imagination	*Remote Associates Test* (RAT):	
	Measurements:	30 is top score. 21 on the RAT equals 7 on the Personalysis for Cognition. 7+ indicates high ideational flow.
	—Ideational flow.	
	—Ideational flexibility.	
III. Memory	*Weschler Memory Test* (WMT):	
	Measurements:	118 is top score. 83 on the WMT equals 7 on the Personalysis for Cognition. 7+ indicates high retention.
	—Personal and current information.	
	—Orientation.	
	—Mental control.	
	—Logical memory.	
	—Digits.	
	—Visual reproduction.	
	—Associate learning.	
IV. Humor	*Humor Scale #5* (HS) (from Social Intelligence Test):	
	Measurements:	20 is top score. 14 on the HS equals 7 on the Personalysis for Cognition. 7+ indicates a high degree of wit.
	—Sense of humor.	
	—Range of humor.	

Back-up Chart for Cognition (*continued*)

Factors to be Considered:	Sample Instruments:	Conversion of Scores:
V. Social Intelligence	*Social Intelligence Test* (SIT—2nd Edition): Measurements: —Judgment in social situations. —Recognition of mental state of speaker. —Memory for names and faces. —Observation of human behavior. —Sense of humor.	160 is top score. 112 on SIT equals 7 on the Personalysis for Cognition. 7+ indicates a high degree of social intelligence.

Back-up Chart for Affect

Factors to be Considered:	Sample Instruments:	Conversion of Scores:
I. Empathy	*Observation Technique:* Measurements: —Student's ability to comprehend the feelings, thoughts, and motives of others.	Altruistic or empathetic behavior is displayed 70 percent of the time when interacting with others. 70 percent equals 7 on the Personalysis for Affect. 7+ indicates high degrees of empathy.

Back-up Chart for Affect (*continued*)

Factors to be Considered:	Sample Instruments:	Conversion of Scores:
II. Sensitivity	*Observation Technique:*	
	Measurements: —Student's ability to respond quickly to internal and external stimuli, especially the attitudes, feelings, or circumstances of self and others.	Sensitive behavior is exhibited 70 percent of the time when confronted with stimuli. 70 percent equals 7 on the Personalysis for Affect. 7+ indicates high degrees of sensitivity.
III. Temperament	*The Sixteen Factor Personality Test* (16-FPT):	
	Measurements: —Reserved—outgoing. —Less intelligent—more intelligent. —Affected by feelings—emotionally stable. —Humble—assertive. —Sober—happy go lucky. —Expedient—conscientious. —Shy—venturesome. —Tough-minded—tender-minded. —Trusting—suspicious. —Practical—imaginative. —Forthright—shrewd.	Raw scores on the 16-FPT are converted to sten scores (stens). A composite sten score of 7 or above equals 7 on the Personalysis for Affect. 7+ indicates a high degree of positive temperament traits.

—Placid—
apprehensive.
—Conservative—
experimentive.
—Group-dependent—
self-sufficient.
—Undisciplined—
controlled.
—Relaxed—tense.

Back-up Chart for Conation

Factors to be Considered:	Sample Instrument or Observation Techniques:	Conversion of Scores:
I. Interests	*Kuder Preference Record-Personal* (KPR-P—Form AH/Score C):	
	Measurements:	96 is top score. 67 on the KPR equals 7 on the Personalysis for Conation. 7+ indicates a strong preference for working with ideas.
	—Score C measures a preference for working with ideas. A high score indicates that a person is interested in ideas and philosophizing. There is a distinct preference for situations in which he or she can think about ideas and problems rather than work with things.	

Back-up Chart for Conation (*continued*)

Factors to be Considered:	Sample Instrument or Observation Techniques:	Conversion of Scores:
II. Motivation	*Observation Technique:*	
	Measurements:	The initiation and completion of seven projects or tasks during the academic year equals 7 on the Personalysis for Conation. 7+ indicates a high degree of motivation/task commitment.
	—Student-initiated projects, contracts, or tasks as observed by the DEG educationist.	
III. Curiosity	*Observation Technique:*	
	Measurements:	70 percent of the questions posed are student-initiated. 70 percent equals 7 on the Personalysis for Conation. 7+ indicates a high degree of curiosity.
	—Student-initiated questioning about relevant problems, concepts, issues, or ideas in which he or she takes quite frequently an antithetical position as observed by the DEG educationist.	

Appendix B
PROGRAM EVALUATION FOR DEG

APPLICATION OF THE THREE MATRICES FOR DEG PROGRAM EVALUATION

The following three evaluative matrices link Ward's, prescriptive theory (1980) with three practical evaluation devices that address three distinct levels of educational decision-making:

    I. The normative level (policy formulation)
    II. The tactical level (policy implementation)
    III. The strategical level (program operation).

Each program requirement (Ward's axioms) has a set of three specific requisites (Ward's corollaries) that are connected with the four key factors or features found in the DEG taxonomy. These specific program requisites are self-explanatory and are followed by a practical rating device with three evaluative considerations.

    (1) The presence of an important corollary (+1)
    (2) The partial presence of a corollary (0)
    (3) The absence of a corollary (−1).

An ideal program for the gifted would, therefore, operate on a (+36), an average program between a (−12) to (+12) spread, and an antithetical setting for the gifted on a (−36) rating. These ratings set standards: they help us validate giftedness psychometrically, assist us in planning an articulated and differentiated curriculum, and tell us more about the methods to

A MATRIX OF CRITERIA FOR THE EVALUATION OF DEG PROGRAMS
(Partially adopted from Renzulli and Ward, 1969)

Decision-Making Levels (Here: I)	Theoretic Key Features (A.–D.)	General Program Requirements (IA.–ID.)	Specific Program Requisites (IA. (a–c)—ID. (a–c))	RATINGS Present (+1)	Partially Present (0)	Absent (−1)
I. The Normative Level (i.e., Policy Formulation)	A. Gifted Student	IA. Validity of Conception and Adequacy of Procedures	IA. a. Conceptions of giftedness (g-factor) and Aptitudes (s-factors)			
			b. Culture-fair identification procedures of g-factor and s-factors			
			c. Placement of students			
	B. DEG Educationist	IB. Validity of Conception and Adequacy of Procedures	IB. a. Conceptions of generalists (i.e., nurture of g-factor) and specialists (i.e., nurture of s-factors)			
			b. Selection and training procedures			
			c. Placement of generalists and specialists			

C. Demands of Knowledge

IC. Validity of Conception and Adequacy of Procedures

IC. a. Conceptions of generative and terminal knowledge
b. Curricular differentiation
c. Generative knowledge in all epistemological classes

D. Needs of Society

ID. Validity of Conception and Adequacy of Philosophy

ID. a. Conceptions of democracy and pragmatism in the context of DEG
b. Philosophical consistency with democracy and pragmatism
c. Philosophical consistency with reconstructionism

SUBTOTAL:

A MATRIX OF CRITERIA FOR THE EVALUATION OF DEG PROGRAMS—CON'T.
(Partially adopted from Renzulli and Ward, 1969)

RATINGS

Decision-Making Levels (Here: II)	Theoretic Key Features (A.–D.)	General Program Requirements (IIA.–IID.)	Specific Program Requisites (IIA. (a–c)—IID. (a–c))	Present (+1)	Partially Present (0)	Absent (−1)
II. The Tactical Level (i.e., Policy Implementation)	A. Gifted Student	IIA. Roles and Responsibilities	IIA. a. Opportunities for democratic leadership and social reconstruction			
			b. Opportunities for knowledge production (KP)			
			c. Provisions for evaluative feedback to all decision-making levels			
	B. DEG Educationist	IIB. Roles and Responsibilities	IIB. a. Opportunities for leadership and social reconstructionism in and out of school			
			b. Emphasis on knowledge production in all epistemological classes			
			c. Provisions for evaluative feedback to all decision-making levels			

C. Demands of Knowledge	IIC. Adequacy of Facilities and Resources	a. Centrality of instructional facilities and resources			
		b. Availability of facilities and resources			
		c. Provisions for evaluative feedback on achievement of gifted students and DEG educationists			
D. Needs of Society	IID. Program Organization within an Existing School System	a. Existence of a document that states purpose, design, substance, and predicted outcome of the program			
		b. Administrative responsibilities and financial allocation			
		c. Provisions for evaluative feedback to all decision-making levels			

SUBTOTAL:

A MATRIX OF CRITERIA FOR THE EVALUATION OF DEG PROGRAMS—CONT.

(Partially adopted from Renzulli and Ward, 1969)

Decision-Making Levels (Here: III)	Theoretic Key Features (A.–D.)	General Program Requirements (IIIA.–IIID.)	Specific Program Requisites (IIIA. (a–c)—IIID. (a–c))	RATINGS Present (+1)	Partially Present (0)	Absent (–1)
III. The Strategic Level (i.e., Program Operation)	A. Gifted Student	IIIA. Appropriateness of Relationship between Capacity and Curriculum	IIIA. a. Required core (g) and range of electives (s)			
			b. Programmatic enrichment, i.e., requirements and electives			
			c. Provisional enrichment, i.e., independent study and contractual work			
	B. DEG Educationist	IIIB. Appropriateness of Relationship between Knowledge and Methodology	IIIB. a. Flexibility of teaching styles			
			b. Content/methods for "educare," i.e., strategies for aptitudinal input			
			c. Content/method for "educere," i.e., strategies for ideational and generative output			

C. Demands of Knowledge

IIIC. Comprehensiveness and Articulation
- a. Curricular design and objectives
- b. Consistency with overall program of general education
- c. Developmental objectives and characterology

D. Needs of Society

IIID. Public Relations
- a. Communal assessment of attitudes toward the program
- b. Strategies for attitudinal change
- c. Strategies for public involvement and support

SUBTOTALS:

GRAND TOTAL:

be employed to advocate a program for the gifted in the democratic context.

Jellen, H. 1981. Programme evaluation in differential education for the gifted (DEG). *New Horizons in Education: The Journal of the World Education Fellowship in Australia* 65:26–32.

Appendix C
UNIT CONSTRUCTION FOR DEG

APPLICATION OF UNIT CONSTRUCTION FOR DEG

Unit construction for DEG implies qualitative differentiation of contents and methods that have particular relevance to DEG, as well as sequential articulation.

Qualitative differentiation of contents is a demand for generative types of knowledge which have the potential for knowledge production to occur and can be found in all content areas listed in the taxonomy. Ward et al. (1962) list six types of generative knowledge which should be considered for unit construction of curricular contents suited for DEG.

1. Functional Concepts: Functional concepts must be useful to the gifted learner in current thought and learning processes. They have the potential for desirable maturation and intellectual challenge.

2. Great Ideas: Great ideas are significant abstractions which have contributed to epistemological progress in all academic disciplines.

3. Perspectives Upon Knowledge: This type of generative knowledge should explore entire fields and systems of knowledge—their linkages, gaps, and unknowns. An exploration of this sort is a study *about* subjects rather than *of* subjects.

4. Significant Theses: A study of existing paradigms, theorems, hypotheses, causes, and effects advanced enough in complexity of thought beyond the level feasible for students who are not exceptionally endowed.

5. Hidden Realities: Potential influences in the determination of personal conduct or social action and development; these "realities" are not readily apparent but substantially real with possible social or personal impact.

6. Summary Analyses: These varied abstractions, groupings, ratings, summaries, and/or evaluations of facts, principles, and ideas must cut across content boundaries, fields of knowledge, or human achievements.

Parallel to qualitative differentiation of contents runs the demand for qualitative differentiation of methods which should emphasize "educere" (Lat. "the leading out of") as a pedagogical means to reinforce and encourage intellectual autonomy on the part of the gifted learner. The six pedagogical approaches chosen for and discussed in this handbook have the greatest potential to trigger independent and exploratory thought necessary for knowledge production to take place.

1. Discovery Approach
2. Games/Play Approach
3. Interest Approach
4. Polytechnical Approach
5. Problem Approach
6. Systems Approach.

Both DEG contents and DEG methods are sequentially articulated from a more concrete or basic understanding of a concept or an idea to a more complex, abstract, or evaluative notion of a given thesis. The following two sample sheets offer the reader an examplary illustration of sequential articulation (that is, degrees of difficulty or complexity ranked from 1 through 12) *and* qualitative differentiation of DEG contents (top part of the chart) as well as DEG methods (bottom part of the chart). "Ethics" was chosen as a content area representing the curricular core; "empirics" was chosen as a content area representing the curricular electives. Both core and electives should contribute to programmatic enrichment of the gifted.

Partially adapted from Ward, V. et al. 1962. *The gifted student: A manual for program improvement*, 49–70. Atlanta: Southern Regional Education Board.

Unit Construction

LIFETIME LEARNING

CURRICULAR CONTENTS	
12 Summary Analysis:	12 Choosing Righteousness and Goodness.
11 Hidden Realities in Ethics:	11 Virtues and Character.
10 Hidden Realities in Ethics:	10 The Rewards of Goodness.
9 Hidden Realities in Ethics:	9 Moral Dilemmas.
8 Significant Theses in Ethics:	8 Moral Codes.
7 Significant Theses in Ethics:	7 Selflessness and Selfishness.
6 Great Ideas in Ethics:	6 Self-Actualization and Self-Realization.
5 Perspectives on Ethical Theories:	5 Authoritarianism, Intuition, Empiricism, and Reason.
4 Functional Concepts in Ethics:	4 Right/Wrong and Good/Evil.
3 Functional Concepts in Ethics:	3 Free Will and Autonomy.
2 Functional Concepts in Ethics:	2 Methods and Theories.
1 Perspectives on Ethics:	1 The Field of Ethics in the Context of Philosophy.

EPISTEMO-LOGICAL CLASSES & BRANCHES

EX.: ETHICS	EX.: MORAL DEVELOPMENT

PEDAGOGICAL METHODS	
1 Discovery Approach:	1 Ethics as a Branch of Philosophy.
2 Systems Approach:	2 Types of Ethical Methods and Theories.
3 Problem Approach:	3 The Problem of Choice.
4 Problem Approach:	4 The Problem of Determining Right/Wrong and Good/Evil.
5 Discovery Approach:	5 Goodness in Authoritarianism, Intuition, Empiricism, and Reason.
6 Discovery Approach:	6 The Freedom of the Self.
7 Discovery Approach:	7 Analysis of Motives.
8 Discovery Approach:	8 Analysis of Moral Codes.
9 Games/Play Approach:	9 Simulations with Moral Dilemmas.
10 Discovery Approach:	10 Biographical Studies of Virtues in Genius.
11 Discovery Approach:	11 Self- and Peer Evaluation According to Virtues.
12 Interest Approach:	12 Contract to do Something Good for Someone Else.

LIFETIME LEARNING

LIFETIME LEARNING

CURRICULAR CONTENTS		
12 Summary Analyses for Scientific Methods:	12 Evaluations of Reality Testing in All "Scientific Methods."	
11 Summary Analyses for Empirics:	11 Evaluations of Factuality, Reality, and Actuality.	
10 Hidden Realities in Scientific Methods:	10 The Uses and Abuses of Scientific Methods.	
9 Hidden Realities in Empirics:	9 The Uses and Abuses of Science.	
8 Significant Theses in Scientific Methods:	8 Reality Testing.	
7 Significant Theses in Empirics:	7 Evolution vs. Creationism.	
6 Great Ideas in Scientific Methods:	6 Data and Taxonomy.	
5 Great Ideas in Empirics:	5 Evidence and Testing.	
4 Functional Concepts in Scientific Methods:	4 Variable and Hypothesis.	
3 Functional Concepts in Empirics:	3 Measurement and Method.	
2 Perspectives on Scientific Methods:	2 Types of Methodology That Contribute to Scientific Inquiry.	
1 Perspectives on Empirics:	1 Fields of Knowledge That Contribute to Science.	

EPISTEMO-LOGICAL CLASSES & BRANCHES

EX.: EMPIRICS   EX.: SCIENTIFIC METHOD

PEDAGOGICAL METHODS		
1 Systems Approach:	1 Types of "Science."	
2 Systems Approach:	2 Types of "Scientific Methods."	
3 Systems Approach:	3 Types of Measuring.	
4 Problem Approach:	4 Identification of Variables and Stating of Hypotheses.	
5 Discovery Approach:	5 Testing of Evidence.	
6 Problem Approach:	6 Classification of Relevant Data.	
7 Discovery Approach:	7 The Confirmation or Refutation of Evolution or Creationism.	
8 Discovery Approach:	8 The Metaphysics of Experimentalism.	
9 Discovery Approach:	9 The Axiology of Experimentalism.	
10 Problem Approach:	10 The Falsification of Variables, Hypotheses, and Data.	
11 Systems Approach:	11 Factuality, Reality, and Actuality in All Fields of Science.	
12 Systems Approach:	12 Assessment of Types of Reality According to Types of Scientific Methods.	

LIFETIME LEARNING

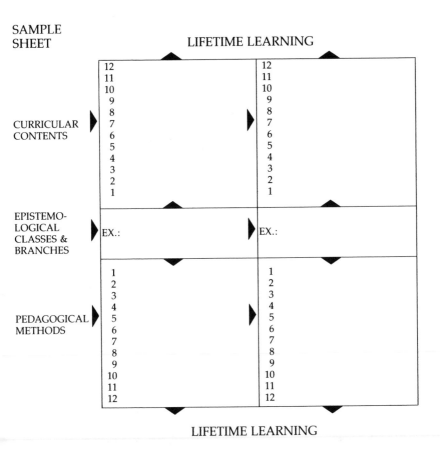

SAMPLE
SHEET

LIFETIME LEARNING

CURRICULAR
CONTENTS

12
11
10
9
8
7
6
5
4
3
2
1

12
11
10
9
8
7
6
5
4
3
2
1

EPISTEMO-
LOGICAL
CLASSES &
BRANCHES

EX.:

EX.:

PEDAGOGICAL
METHODS

1
2
3
4
5
6
7
8
9
10
11
12

1
2
3
4
5
6
7
8
9
10
11
12

LIFETIME LEARNING

Appendix D
MENTAL TESTING IN DEG

APPLICATION OF MENTAL TESTING IN DEG

Psychology and psychometrics have made great strides in the measurement of intelligence in general and the g-factor (that is, general innate mental ability) in particular. Unfortunately, the *Zeitgeist* of education is so utterly egalitarian and pessimistic concerning the administration of culture-fair IQ tests that highly questionable identification procedures have replaced valid and reliable psychometric instruments designed to measure mental ability. The mere mentioning of the IQ-metric triggers suspicion and prejudice among those educators who contend that all children have "gifts."

Despite such accommodating and self-defeating claims for freeing the mental construct of giftedness from its one-sided attachment to the IQ-metric, the essential point remains: In research as in educational practice, the individualized IQ-metric has been and will continue to be the most accurate, objective, and predominant criterion in identifying highly gifted students (Eysenck, 1979).

Individualized and culture-fair IQ batteries which recognize outstanding cognitive behavior as accurate recall (memory), as speedy discovery (ideational flow and production), and as sound evaluation (critical judgment) in relevant problem-solving situations promise to make the greatest contribution to our efforts in identifying "low incidents" or the highly gifted. Since the individualized IQ-metric has been proven not only to be valid but also reliable in the identification of degrees of mental retardation, one can only be surprised to find suspicion among educators when it is applied to the identification of degrees of giftedness. Psychometric illiteracy seems to run high in educational circles.

A balance between traditional and nontraditional assessment techniques will provide additional information on the noncognitive qualities in the affective *and* conative domains of a gifted mind. Nevertheless, the *mental* construct of "gifted mind" must maintain its centrality in our psychometric efforts to identify, to understand, and to educate gifted children in general and low incidents in particular.

The chart on the following page lists traditional and nontraditional assessment techniques which have been proven effective in creating a talent-pool of promising students from all socio-economic and ethnic backgrounds for DEG programs. The application of the individualized IQ battery, administered by a trained psychologist, must remain, however, the last screening device for inclusion in or exclusion from a given DEG program.

Sources:

Buros, O., ed. 1970. *Personality: Tests and reviews.* Vols. 1–3. Highland Park, NJ: Gryphon Press.

Eysenck, H. 1979. *The nature and measurement of intelligence.* New York: Springer.

Traditional Assessment Techniques for the Identification of Exceptionality

Cognitive Domain	Affective Domain	Conative Domain
* Individualized IQ Batteries.	* Temperament Surveys.	* Interest Inventories.
* Scholastic/Academic Achievement Tests.	* Personality Assessment Scales.	* Leadership Ability Evaluation.
* Mental Scales.	* Attitudinal Scales.	* Motivational Scales.
* Humor Scales.	* Values Inventories.	* Aspiration Scales.
* Tests on Social Insights.	* Diplomacy Test of Empathy.	

Non-traditional or Culture-fair Assessment Techniques for the Identification of Exceptionality

Cognitive Domain	Affective Domain	Conative Domain
* Observation Techniques.	* Observation Techniques.	* Observation Techniques.
* Competitive Gaming; for example, chess, WFF N proof; equations; transfigurations.	* Self Evaluations.	* Volunteerism.
	* Peer Evaluations.	* Monitorism.
	* Self Nominations.	* Mentorships.
* College Bowls.	* Peer Nominations.	* Tutorships.
* Auditions.		

ANNOTATED BIBLIOGRAPHY

Gowan, J. 1961. *An annotated bibliography on the academically talented*. Washington: National Education Association of the United States.

Laubenfels, J. 1977. *The gifted student: An annotated bibliography*. Westport, CT: Greenwood Press.

Start, A. 1972. *The gifted child: A select annotated bibliography*. Windsor, England: National Foundation for Educational Research in England and Wales.

REFERENCE BOOKS

Arnold, W. et al., eds. 1976. *Lexikon der Psychologie*. Vols. 1–3. Freiburg, West Germany: Herder.

Baldwin, J. 1960. *Dictionary of philosophy and psychology*. Vols. 1–3. Gloucester, England: Smith.

Buisson, F. 1911. *Nouveau dictionnaire de pédagogie et d'instruction primaire*. Paris, France: Librairie Hachette.

Castillo, C., and O. Bond, eds. 1973. *Spanish-English, English-Spanish dictionary*. New York: Pocket Books.

Castonguay, J. 1973. *Dictionnaire de la psychologie et des sciences connexes (Français-Anglais)*. Paris, France: Maloine.

Cerezo, S., ed. 1970. *Enciclopedia técnica de la educación*. Vols. 1–3. Madrid, Spain: Santillana.

Drever, J. 1964. *A dictionary of psychology*. Baltimore: Penguin.

Duijker, H., and M. Rijswijk, eds. 1975. *Trilingual psychological dictionary: English, German, French*. Vols. 1–3. Bern, Switzerland: Huber.

Edwards, P., ed. 1967. *The encyclopedia of philosophy*. Vols. 1–8. New York: Macmillan.

English, H., and A. English. 1958. *A comprehensive dictionary of psychological and psychoanalytical terms*. New York: McKay.

Fairchild, H., ed. 1944. *Dictionary of sociology.* New York: Philosophical Library.

Foulquie, P. 1971. *Dictionnaire de la langue pédagogique.* Paris, France: Presses Universitaires de France.

————. 1978. *Dictionnaire de la langue philosophique.* 3rd ed. Paris, France: Presses Universitaires de France.

Garmonsway, G., and J. Simpson, 1969. *The Penguin English dictionary.* Harmondsworth, England: Penguin.

Glosario de términos utilizados en estadística educativa. 1974. Santiago, Chile: Centro Interamericano de Ensenanza.

Good, C., ed. 1959. *Dictionary of education.* New York: McGraw-Hill.

————. 1973. *Dictionary of education.* 3rd ed. New York: McGraw-Hill.

Gould, J., and W. Kolb, eds., 1964. *A dictionary of the social sciences.* New York: Macmillan.

Herderbücherei. *Wörterbuch der pädagogischen Psychologie.* Freiburg, West Germany: Herder.

Herrmann, T. et al., eds. 1977. *Handbuch psychologischer Grundbegriffe.* Munich, West Germany: Kösel Verlag.

Hotyat, F. et al. 1973. *Dictionnaire encyclopédique de pédagogie moderne.* Paris, France: Nathan.

Hutchins, R., and M. Adler, eds. 1952. *Great books of the western world (a syntopicon).* Chicago: Encyclopedia Britannica.

Kernig, C., ed. 1972. *Marxism, communism, and western society.* Vols. 1–8. New York: Herder and Herder.

Krings, H. et al., eds. 1973. *Handbuch philosophischer Grundbegriffe.* Vols. 1–3. Munich, West Germany: Kösel Verlag.

Lafon, R. 1979. *Vocabulaire de psychopédagogie et de psychiatrie de l'enfant.* 4th ed. Paris, France: Presses Universitaîres de France.

Messinger, H., and W. Rüdenberg, eds. 1964. *Langenscheidts Handwörterbuch: Englisch-Deutsch und Deutsch-Englisch.* Vols. 1–2. Berlin, West Germany: Langenscheidt.

Minot, J. 1974. *Lexique des termes en usage dans l'administration de l'education.* Paris, France: Institut National d'Administration Scolaire et Universitaire.

Moor, L. 1969. *English-French-German glossary for psychiatry, child psychiatry and abnormal psychology.* Paris, France: L'Expansion Scientifique Française.

Page, G. et al. 1977. *International dictionary of education*. London: Kogan Page.

Ritter, J. et al., eds. 1971. *Historisches Wörterbuch der Philosophie*. Vols. 1–5. Stuttgart, West Germany: Schwabe.

Rombach, H. ed. 1977. *Wörterbuch der Pädagogik*. Vols. 1–3. Freiburg, West Germany: Herder.

Sills, D., ed. 1968. *International encyclopedia of social sciences*. Vols. 1–18. New York: Macmillan.

Smith, C. et al. 1971. *Collins Spanish-English, English-Spanish dictionary*. London: Collins.

Speck, J., and G. Wehle, eds. 1970. *Handbuch pädagogischer Grundbegriffe*. Vols. 1–2. Munich, West Germany: Kösel Verlag.

Weber, E. et al. 1974. *Kleines sozialwissenschaftliches Wörterbuch für Pädagogen*. Donauwörth, West Germany: Auer.

Wolker, W. et al. 1973. *A glossary of educational terms: Usage in five English-speaking countries*. St. Lucia, Australia: University of Queensland Press.

BOOKS

Abraham, W. 1958. *Commonsense about gifted children*. New York: Harper and Row.

Ackoff, R., and F. Emery. 1972. *On purposeful systems*. London: Tavistock.

Adler, M. 1982. *The paideia proposal*. New York: Macmillan.

Allen, S. 1978. *Meeting of minds*. New York: Crown Publishers.

Allport, G. 1937. *Personality: A psychological interpretation*. New York: Holt.

Annett, J., ed. 1974. *Psychometrics*. Milton Keynes, England: The Open University Press.

Arasten, A. 1968. *Creativity in the life cycle*. Vols. 1–2. Leiden, Netherlands: Brill.

Arieti, S. 1976. *Creativity: The magic synthesis*. New York: Basic.

Assagioli, R. 1971. *The act of will*. New York: Penguin.

Atkinson, J., and N. Feather, eds. 1966. *A theory of achievement motivation*. New York: Wiley.

Axline, V. 1964. *Dibs: In search of self*. Harmondsworth, England: Penguin.

Barbe, W., and J. Renzulli, eds. 1975. *Psychology and education of the gifted*. New York: Irvington.

Barron, F. 1972. *Artists in the making*. New York: Seminar Press.

Bennett, A., and C. Baylis. 1939. *Formal logic: A modern introduction*. New York: Prentice Hall.

Bentley, A. 1966. *Musical ability*. London: Harrap.

Berlin, I. 1979. *Concepts and categories*. New York: Viking.

Bernstein, B. 1974. *Class, codes and control*. Vol. 1. London: Routledge and Kegan.

Bindra, D., and J. Stewart, eds. 1971. *Motivation*. Harmondsworth, England: Penguin.

Bingham, W. 1937. *Aptitudes and aptitude testing*. New York: Harper.

Birch, J., and E. Williams. 1955. *Challenging gifted children*. New York: Public School Publishers.

Bloom, B. et al. 1956. *Taxonomy of educational objectives: The classification of educational goals* (Handbook I: The cognitive domain). New York: McKay.

Blurton-Jones, N. 1972. *Ethnological studies of child behavior*. Cambridge, England: Cambridge University Press.

Boocock, S., and E. Schild, eds. 1968. *Simulation games in learning*. Beverly Hills, CA: Sage.

Branch, M., and A. Cash. 1966. *Gifted children*. London: Souvenir Press.

Brandwin, P. 1955. *The gifted student as a future scientist*. New York: Harcourt Brace.

Brody, E., and N. Brody. 1976. *Intelligence: Nature, determinants, and consequences*. New York: Academic Press.

Bruner, J. 1960. *The process of education*. Cambridge, MA: Harvard University Press.

Bruner, J. et al., eds. 1976. *Play: Its role in development and evolution*. Harmondsworth, England: Penguin.

Buber, M. 1958. *I and thou*. New York: Charles Scribner's Sons.

Buckley, W. 1967. *Sociology and modern system theory*. Englewood Cliffs, NJ: Prentice-Hall.

Buros, O., ed. 1961. *Tests in print*. Highland Park, NJ: Gryphon Press.

———. 1970. *Personality tests and reviews*. Highland Park, NJ: Gryphon Press.

————. 1975. *Intelligence tests and reviews*. Highland Park, NJ: Gryphon Press.

————. 1978. *The eighth mental measurements yearbook*. Vols. 1–2. Highland Park, NJ: Gryphon Press.

Burt, C. 1975. *The gifted child*. London: Hodder and Stoughton.

Button, L. 1971. *Discovery and experience*. London: Oxford University Press.

Butts, R. 1955. *A cultural history of western education*. New York: McGraw-Hill.

Cassidy, H. 1969. *Knowledge, experience and action*. New York: Columbia Teachers College Press.

Castillo, G. 1974. *Left-handed teaching: Lessons in affective education*. New York: Praeger.

Cattell, R. 1971. *Abilities: Their structure, growth, and action*. Boston: Houghton-Mifflin.

Chaplin, J., and T. Krawiec. 1960. *Systems and theories of psychology*. New York: Holt, Rinehart and Winston.

Clark, B. 1979. *Growing up gifted*. Columbus, OH: Merrill.

Cobb, E. 1977. *The ecology of imagination in childhood*. London: Routledge and Kegan.

Cohen, M., and E. Nagel. 1934. *An introduction to logic and scientific method*. New York: Harcourt and Brace.

Covington, M. et al. 1974. *The productive thinking program. A course in learning to think*. Columbus, OH: Merrill.

Covington, M., and R. Beery. 1976. *Self-worth and school learning*. New York: Holt, Rinehart and Winston.

Cronbach, L., and R. Snow. 1977. *Aptitudes and instructional methods*. New York: Irvington.

Cubberly, E. 1919. *Public education in the United States*. Boston: Houghton Mifflin.

Davis, G. 1973. *Psychology of problem solving*. New York: Basic Books.

Davis, G., and J. Scott. 1971. *Training creative thinking*. New York: Rinehart and Winston.

Davison, A., and P. Gordon. 1978. *Games and simulations in action*. London: Woburn Press.

DeBono, E. 1972. *Children solve problems*. London: Allen Lane.

Dennis, W., and M. Dennis, eds., 1976. *The intellectually gifted: An overview*. New York: Grune and Stratton.

Dewey, J. 1910. *How we think*. Boston: Heath.

———. 1916. *Democracy and education*. New York: Macmillan.

———. 1969. *Interest and effort in education*. Bath, England: Chivers.

Elliot, R. 1976. *Imagination: "A kind of magical faculty."* Birmingham, England: University of Birmingham Press.

Ellis, A., and R. Harper. 1961. *A guide to rational living*. Englewood Cliffs, NJ: Prentice-Hall.

Emery, F., ed. 1969. *Systems thinking*. Harmondsworth, England: Penguin.

Erikson, F. 1964. *Insight and responsibility*. New York: Norton.

Eysenck, H. 1976. *The measurement of personality*. Lancaster, England: Medical and Technical Publishing Co.

———. 1979. *The nature and measurement of intelligence*. New York: Springer.

Feuerstein, R. 1979. *Instrumental enrichment program*. Baltimore, MD: University Park Press.

Fliegler, L. 1961. *Curriculum planning for the gifted*. Englewood Cliffs, NJ: Prentice-Hall.

Forty-ninth yearbook of the National Society for the Study of Education. Part I. 1950. Chicago: University of Chicago Press.

Freehill, M. 1961. *Gifted children: Their psychology and education*. New York: Macmillan.

Freeman, J. 1979. *Gifted children*. Lancaster, England: MTP Press.

French, J., ed. 1959. *Educating the gifted: A book of readings*. New York: Holt, Rinehart and Winston.

Fryer, D. 1931. *The measurement of interests*. New York: Holt, Rinehart and Winston.

Gagné, R. 1977. *The conditions of learning*. 3rd ed. New York: Holt, Rinehart and Winston.

Gallagher, J. 1975. *Teaching the gifted child*. Boston: Allyn and Bacon.

Geertzel, V., and M. Geertzel. 1962. *Cradles of eminence*. Boston: Little and Brown.

Gerth, H., and C. Mills. 1953. *Character and social structure*. New York: Harcourt, Brace and World.

Getzels, J., and P. Jackson. 1962. *Creativity and intelligence*. London: Wiley.

Gibson, J., and B. Chennells, eds. 1976. *Gifted children: Looking to their future*. London: Latimer and NAG.

Gold, M. 1965. *Education of the intellectually gifted*. Columbus, OH: Merrill.

Gordon, A. 1949. *Your creative power*. New York: Scribner.

Gordon, W. 1961. *Synectics: The development of creative capacity*. New York: Harper and Row.

Gowen, D. et al., eds. 1967. *Creativity: Its educational implications*. New York: Wiley.

Grinker, R., ed. 1965. *Toward a unified theory of human behavior*. London: Basic Books.

Guilford, J. 1954. *Psychometric methods*. New York: McGraw-Hill.

———. 1967. *The nature of human intelligence*. New York: McGraw-Hill.

———. 1968. *Intelligence, creativity, and educational implications*. San Diego, CA: Knapp.

Guilford, J., and R. Hoepfner. 1971. *The analysis of intelligence*. New York: McGraw-Hill.

Hagen, E. 1980. *Identification of the gifted*. New York: Teachers College Press.

Hall, R. 1956. *Gifted children: The Cleveland story*. Cleveland, OH: World Publishers.

Havighurst, R., and H. Taba. 1949. *Adolescent character and personality*. New York: John Wiley and Sons.

Havighurst, R. et al. 1955. *A survey of the education of gifted children*. Chicago: Chicago University Press.

Heckhausen, H. 1967. *The anatomy of achievement motivation*. New York: Academic Press.

Heilbroner, R. 1974. *An inquiry into the human prospect*. New York: Norton.

Hildreth, G. et al. 1952. *Educating gifted children at Hunter College elementary school*. New York: Harper and Row.

Hildreth, G. 1966. *Introduction to the gifted*. New York: McGraw-Hill.

Hitchfield, E. 1973. *In search of promise*. London: Longman.

Hollingworth, L. 1926. *Gifted children: Their nature and nurture*. New York: Macmillan.

———. 1942. *Children above 180 IQ*. New York: Harcourt and Brace.

———. 1942. *Children who tested above 180 IQ Stanford Binet: Origin and development*. New York: World Book.

Holton, G. 1978. *The scientific imagination*. London: Cambridge University Press.

Hopkinson, D. 1978. *The education of gifted children*. London: Woburn Press.

Horn, R., ed. 1977. *The guide to simulation games for education and training*. Lexington, KY: Information Resources.

Hudson, L. 1965. *Intelligence: Convergent and divergent*. London: Penguin Science Survey.

Husen, T. 1974. *Talent, equality and meritocracy: Availability and utilization of talent*. The Hague, Netherlands: Nijoff.

Jackson, S. 1971. *A teacher's guide to tests and testing*. London: Longman.

James, W. 1911. *Talks to teachers on psychology: And to students on some of life's ideals*. London: Longman.

Jencks, C. 1980. *Who gets ahead?* New York: Basic.

Johnson, D. 1972. *A systematic introduction to the psychology of thinking*. New York: Harper and Row.

Jones, L. 1980. *Great expectations*. New York: Ballantine.

Keating, D., ed. 1976. *Intellectual talent: Research and development*. Baltimore, MD: Johns Hopkins University Press.

Klages, L. 1929. *The science of character*. London: Allen and Unwin.

Klausmeier, H. et al. 1974. *Conceptual learning and development: A cognitive view*. New York: Academic Press.

Kleinmuntz, B., ed. 1966. *Problem-solving: Research, method, and theory*. New York: Wiley.

Kline, P. 1979. *Psychometrics and psychology*. London: Academic Press.

Koestler, A. 1964. *The act of creation*. New York: Macmillan.

Körner, S. 1955. *Conceptual thinking: A logical inquiry*. Cambridge, England: Cambridge University Press.

Krathwohl, D. et al. 1964. *Taxonomy of educational objectives: The classification of educational goals* (Handbook II: The affective domain). New York: McKay.

Kwalwasser, J. 1955. *Exploring the musical mind*. New York: Coleman-Ross.

Larrabee, H. 1945. *Reliable knowledge*. Boston: Houghton Mifflin.

Laycock, S. 1957. *Gifted children: A handbook for the classroom teacher*. Toronto, Canada: Copp-Clark.

Lazarus, A. 1971. *Behavior therapy and beyond*. New York: McGraw-Hill.

Lee, V., and P. Williams, eds. 1972. *Creativity*. Milton Keynes, England: The Open University Press.

Lesgold, E. et al. 1978. *Cognitive psychology and instruction*. New York: Plenum.

Lewis, M., and L. Rosenblum. 1978. *The development of affect*. New York: Plenum.

Lieberman, J. 1977. *Playfulness*. New York: Academic Press.

Light, P. 1979. *The development of social sensitivity*. Cambridge, England: Cambridge University Press.

Ligon, E. 1948. *A greater generation*. New York: Macmillan.

Lipman, M. et al. 1980. *Philosophy in the classroom*. 2nd ed. Philadelphia: Temple University Press.

Lytton, H. 1971. *Creativity and education*. London: Routledge and Kegan.

McClelland, D. et al., eds. 1953. *The achievement motive*. New York: Appleton.

McClelland, D. et al., eds. 1958. *Talent and society*. New York: Van Nostrand.

McClelland, D. 1961. *The achieving society*. Princeton, NJ: Van Nostrand.

McCormick, L. 1920. *Characterology: An exact science*. New York: Rand McNally.

McDougall, W. 1933. *The energies of men*. New York: Scribners.

————. 1960. *An introduction to social psychology*. London: Methuen.

McKellar, P. 1957. *Imagination and thinking*. London: Cohen and West.

Macrae, A. 1933. *Talents and temperaments*. New York: Appleton.

Magoon, R., and H. Jellen. 1980. *Capitalizing on student interests and motivation: The SIU 0-100 Approach*. Poquoson, VA: Human Development Press.

————. 1980. *Leadership development: Democracy in action*. Poquoson, VA: Human Development Press.

Martinson, R. 1974. *The identification of the gifted and talented*. Los Angeles: National/State Leadership Training Institute of the Gifted and Talented.

Maslow, A. 1962. *Toward a psychology of being*. Princeton, NJ: Van Nostrand.

————. 1970. *Motivation and personality*. New York: Harper and Row.

Mead, G. 1964. *On social psychology*. Chicago: Phoenix.

Meeker, M. 1969. *The structure of intellect: Its interpretation and uses*. Columbus, OH: Merrill.

Meltzer, B. et al. 1975. *Symbolic interactionism: Genesis, varieties, and criticism*. London: Routledge.

Millar, S. 1968. *The psychology of play*. Harmondsworth, England: Penguin.

Morgan, H. et al. 1980. *Elementary and secondary level programs for the gifted and talented*. New York: Teachers College Press.

Newell, A., and H. Simon. 1972. *Human problem solving*. Englewood Cliffs, NJ: Prentice-Hall.

Newland, T. E. 1976. *The gifted in socio-educational perspective*. Englewood Cliffs, NJ: Prentice-Hall.

Nossiter, T. et al. 1972. *Imagination and precision in the social sciences*. London: Faber and Faber.

Ogilvie, E. 1973. *Gifted children in primary schools*. London: Macmillan.

Osborn, A. 1963. *Applied imagination*. New York: Scribner.

Osborn, W., and B. Rohan. 1931. *Enriching the curriculum for gifted children*. New York: Macmillan.

Painter, F. 1977. *Gifted children*. Knebworth, England: Painter.

Parnes, S. 1967. *Creative behavior workbook and guidebook*. Vols. 1–2. New York: Scribner.

Passmore, J. 1970. *The perfectability of man*. London: Wyman.

Passow, H. et al. 1955. *Planning for talented youth*. New York: Teachers' College Press.

Peters, R. S. 1959. *Authority, responsibility, and education*. London: Allen and Unwin.

———. 1966. *Ethics and education*. London: Allen and Unwin.

Phenix, P. 1964. *Realms of meaning*. New York: McGraw-Hill.

Piaget, J. 1932. *The moral judgment of the child*. London: Routledge and Kegan.

———. 1950. *The psychology of intelligence*. London: Routledge and Kegan.

Piaget, J. et al. 1973. *Memory and intelligence*. London: Routledge and Kegan.

Plutchick, R. 1980. *Emotion: A psychoevolutionary synthesis*. New York: Harper and Row.

Polanyi, M. 1958. *Personal knowledge*. Chicago: University of Chicago Press.

——. 1966. *The tacit dimension.* Garden City, NJ: Doubleday.

Povet, R., ed. 1980. *Educating the gifted child.* London: Harper and Row.

Pressey, S. 1949. *Educational acceleration: Appraisals and basic problems.* Columbus, OH: Ohio State University Press.

Price, H. 1953. *Thinking and experience.* London: Hutchinson's University Library.

Raths, L. et al. 1978. *Values and teaching.* 2nd ed. Columbus, OH: Merrill.

Ratner, J., ed. 1939. *Intelligence in the modern world.* New York: Modern Library.

Reid, L. 1961. *Ways of knowledge and experience.* New York: Oxford University Press.

Renzulli, J. 1977. *The enrichment triad model.* Storrs, CT: Creative Learning Press.

——. 1980. *The interest-a-lyzer.* Mansfield, CT: Creative Learning Press.

Renzulli, J., and L. Smith. 1978. *The learning styles inventory: A measure of student preference for instructional techniques.* Mansfield, CT: Creative Learning Press.

Resnick, L. 1976. *The nature of intelligence.* New York: Wiley.

Rest, J. 1979. *Development in judging moral issues.* Minneapolis, MN: University of Minnesota Press.

Risenhoover, M., and R. Blackburn. 1976. *Artists as professors: Conversations with musicians, painters, sculptors.* Chicago: University of Illinois Press.

Roback, A. 1952. *The psychology of character.* London: Routledge and Kegan.

Roe, A. 1952. *The making of a scientist.* New York: Dodd and Mead.

Rogers, C. 1969. *Freedom to learn.* Columbus, OH: Merrill.

——. 1975. *Encounter groups.* Harmondsworth, England: Penguin.

Rowland, P. 1974. *Gifted children and their problems.* London: Dent.

Sanderlin, O. 1979. *Gifted children: How to identify and teach them.* South Brunswick: Barnes Press.

Satre, P. 1972. *The psychology of imagination.* London: Methuen.

Scandura, J. et al. 1977. *Problem Solving.* New York: Academic Press.

Scheifele, M. 1953. *The gifted child in the regular classroom.* New York: Teachers' College Press.

Seashore, C. 1938. *Psychology of music*. New York: McGraw-Hill.

Shapovalenko, S., ed. 1963. *Polytechnical education in the U.S.S.R.* Amsterdam, Netherlands: UNESCO.

Shaw, M., and J. Wright. 1967. *Scales for measurement of attitudes*. New York: McGraw-Hill.

Shields, J. 1968. *The gifted child*. Slough, England: NFER Publication.

Simon, S. et al. 1978. *Values clarification*. New York: Visual Library.

Spearman, C. 1927. *The abilities of man*. London: Macmillan.

Stanley, J. et al. 1977. *The gifted and the creative: A fifty-year perspective (1925–1975)*. Baltimore: Johns Hopkins University.

Starmer, G. et al. 1975. *Project method*. Milton Keynes, England: The Open University Press.

Steigman, B. 1964. *Accent on talent*. Detroit, MI: Wayne State University.

Stein, J. 1974. *Stimulating creativity*. Vols 1–3. New York: Academic Press.

Stevens, J. 1971. *Awareness: Exploring, experimenting, experiencing*. New York: Bantam.

Stoddard, G. 1943. *The meaning of intelligence*. New York: Macmillan.

Strongman, K. 1978. *The psychology of emotion*. Chichester, England: Wiley.

Stubbs, M., and S. Delamont. 1976. *Explorations in classroom observation*. London: Wiley.

Sumption, M., and E. Luecking. 1960. *Education of the gifted*. New York: Ronald Press.

Swift, E. 1908. *Mind in the making*. New York: Charles Scribner's Sons.

Taylor, C., ed. 1974. *Climate for creativity*. New York: Pergamon.

Tempest, N. 1974. *Teaching clever children*. London: Routledge and Kegan.

Terman, L. 1925. *Genetic studies of genius (vol. 1): Mental and physical traits of a thousand gifted children*. Stanford, CA: Stanford University Press.

Terman, L., and M. Oden. 1947. *Genetic studies of genius (vol. 4): The gifted child grows up*. Stanford, CA: Stanford University Press.

———. 1959. *Genetic studies of genius (vol. 5): The gifted group at mid-life*. Stanford, CA: Stanford University Press.

Torrance, P. 1962. *Guiding creative talent*. Englewood Cliffs, NJ: Prentice-Hall.

———. 1970. *Encouraging creativity in the classroom*. Dubuque, IA: Brown.

———. 1976. *Guiding creative talent*. 2nd ed. Huntingdon: Krieger Publishing.

Treffinger, D., and C. Curl. 1976. *Self-directed study guide on the education of the gifted and talented*. Ventura, CA: National/State Leadership Training Institute on the Gifted and Talented.

Trower, P. et al. 1978. *Social skill and mental health*. London: Methuen.

Verduin, J. 1967. *Conceptual models in teacher education: An approach to teaching and learning*. Washington: American Association of Colleges for Teacher Education.

Vernon, P., ed. 1970. *Creativity*. Harmondsworth, England: Penguin.

Vernon, P. et al. 1977. *The psychology and education of gifted children*. London: Methuen.

Vernon, W. 1972. *Motivating children*. New York: Holt, Rinehart and Winston.

Wallach, M., and C. Wing. 1969. *The talented student*. New York: Holt, Rinehart and Winston.

Ward, V. 1961. *Educating the gifted: An axiomatic approach*. Columbus, OH: Merrill.

———. 1980. *Differential education for the gifted*. Los Angeles: National/State Leadership Training Institute on the Gifted and Talented.

Warnock, M. 1976. *Imagination*. London: Faber and Faber.

Wertheimer, M. 1945. *Productive thinking*. New York: Harper and Row.

Whitehead, A. 1926. *Religion in the making*. Cambridge, England: Cambridge University Press.

Wicklengren, W. 1974. *How to solve problems*. San Francisco: Freeman.

Witkin, R. 1974. *The intelligence of feeling*. London: Heinemann.

Witty, P., ed. 1951. *The gifted child*. Boston: Heath.

Wolfle, D., ed. 1965. *The discovery of talent*. Cambridge, MA: Harvard University Press.

Wootton, G. 1970. *Interest-groups*. Englewood Cliffs, NJ: Prentice-Hall.

Worcester, D. 1956. *The education of children of above average mentality.* Lincoln, NE: Nebraska University Press.

Wright, D., and M. Croxen, eds. 1976. *Moral development: A cognitive approach.* Milton Keynes, England: The Open University Press.

ARTICLES

Berdie, R. 1946. Interests. In *Encyclopedia of psychology*, ed. Harriman, 305–14. New York: Philosophical Library.

Bernstein, B. 1973. On the classification and framing of educational knowledge. In *Knowledge, education, and cultural change*, ed. Brown, 363–92. London: Tavistock.

Bugental, J., and R. Tannenbaum. 1963. Sensitivity training and being motivated. *Journal of Humanistic Psychology* 3 (1): 76–85.

Clark, K. 1980. Empathy: A neglected topic in psychological research. *American Psychologist* 35 (2): 187–90.

Cooper, E. et al. 1974. Direct observation? *Bulletin of the British Psychological Society* 27 (94): 3–7.

Dellas, M., and E. Gaier. 1975. Identification of creativity: The individual. In *Psychology and education of the gifted*, eds. Barbe and Renzulli, 2nd ed., 195–97. New York: Irvington.

Drake, R. 1946. Aptitude and aptitude training. In *Encyclopedia of psychology*, ed. Harriman, 38–45. New York: Philosophical Library.

Duncker, K. 1945. On problem solving. *Psychological Monograph* 58 (5), no. 270.

Feely, T. 1976. Critical thinking: Toward a definition, paradigm, and research agenda. *Theory and Research in Social Education* 4 (1): 1–19.

Gefferth, E. 1981. Motivation in the background of mathematical talent. *Pszichologia* 2:243–69.

Gibb, C. et al. 1968. Leadership. In *International encyclopedia of social sciences*, ed. Sills, vol. 9, 91–113. New York: Macmillan.

Goleman, D. 1980. 1,528 little geniuses and how they grew. *Psychology Today* 13 (9): 28–67 and 102.

Guilford, J. 1950. Creativity. *The American Psychologist* 5:444–54.

Gustafsson, E. 1981. A unifying model for the structure of intellectual abilities. *Intelligence* 8:179–203.

Heath, C. 1967. Concept. In *The encyclopedia of philosophy*, ed. Edwards, vol. 2, 177–80. New York: Macmillan.

Helson, R. 1971. Women mathematicians and the creative personality. *Journal of Counseling and Clinical Psychology* 36:210–20.

Hoffman, M. 1976. Empathy, role-taking, guilt, and development of altruistic motives. In *Moral development: Current theory and research*, ed. Likona, 180–88. New York: Holt.

Hoffman, M. 1978. Toward a theory of empathic arousal and development. In *The development of affect*. eds. Lewis and Rosenblum, 238–47. New York: Plenum.

Holmes, B. 1965. The reflective man: Dewey. In *The educated man: Studies in the history of educational thought*, eds. Nash et al., 305–34. London: Wiley.

Hutchinson, W. 1967. Creative and productive thinking in the classroom. *Journal of Creative Behavior* 1:419–27.

Isaacs, A. 1973. Giftedness and leadership. *Gifted Child Quarterly* 17 (2): 103–12.

Jellen, H. 1981. Programme evaluation in differential education for the gifted (DEG). *New Horizons in Education* 65:26–32.

———. 1985. Renzulli's enrichment scheme for the gifted: Educational accommodation of the gifted in the American context. *Gifted Education International* 3 (1): 12–17.

———. 1985. The meaning and justifications for DEG in a democracy: A taxonomical approach. *Gifted Education International* 3 (2): 94–99.

Kohlberg, L. 1969. Stage and sequence: The cognitive-developmental approach to socialization. In *Handbook of socialization: Theory and research*, ed. Goslin, 347–480. New York: Rand and McNally.

Kurtines, W., and J. Greif. 1974. The development of moral thought: A review and evaluation of Kohlberg's approach. *Psychological Bulletin* 81 (8): 64–70.

Lundy, J. 1978. The psychological needs of the gifted. *Roeper Review* 1 (2): 5–8.

Magoon, R., and H. Jellen. 1978. The SIU 0-100 approach: An effective way to motivate gifted students. *G/C/T* 3:46–50.

Mansfield, B. et al. 1978. The effectiveness of creativity training. *Review of Educational Research* 48 (4): 517–36.

Norman, D. 1978. Notes toward a theory of complex learning. In

Cognitive psychology and instruction, ed. Lesgold, 39–48. New York: Plenum Press.

Olton, R., and R. Crutchfield. 1969. Developing the skills in productive thinking. In *Trends and issues in developmental psychology*, eds. Mussen et al., 68–91. New York: Holt.

Phillips, M. 1976. Confluent education, the hidden curriculum, and the gifted child. *Phi Delta Kappan* 58 (3): 238–40.

Plutchick, R. 1980. A language for the emotions. *Psychology Today* (Feb.): 68–78.

Renzulli, J. 1978. What makes giftedness? Reexamining a definition. *Phi Delta Kappan* 60 (3): 180–4 and 261.

Renzulli, J. 1980. Will the gifted child movement be alive and well in 1990? *Gifted Child Quarterly* 24:3–9.

Schachter, S., and J. Singer. 1962. Cognitive, social, and physiological determinants of emotional state. *Psychological Review* 69:379–99.

Sonntag, J. 1969. Sensitivity training with gifted children. *Gifted Child Quarterly* 13 (1): 51–7.

Spoerl, H. 1936. Faculties or traits: The solution of Joseph Gall. *Character and Personality* 4:216–31.

Stanley, J. 1973. Accelerating the educational progress of intellectually gifted youth. *Educational Psychologist* 10 (3): 133–46.

Strang, R. 1951. Mental hygiene of gifted children. In *The gifted child*, ed. Witty, 131–62. Boston: Heath.

Suchman, J. 1961. Inquiry training: Building skills for autonomous discovery. *Merrill Palmer Quarterly of Behavior and Development* 7:147–69.

Taba, H. 1963. Learning by discovery: Psychological and educational rationale. *Elementary School Journal* 63:308–16.

Taylor, C., and J. Holland. 1964. Predictors of creative performance. In *Creativity: Progress and Potential*, ed. Taylor, 15–48. New York: McGraw-Hill.

Terman, L. 1954. The discovery and encouragement of exceptional talent. *The American Psychologist* 9:224–30.

Terman, L., and M. Oden. 1954. Major issues in the education of the gifted child. *Journal of Technical Education* 5:230–52.

Torrance, P. 1970. Broadening concepts of giftedness in the 70's. *Gifted Child Quarterly* 14 (4): 199–208.

———. 1976. Give the gifted children of the world a chance to solve future problems. *Talents and Gifts* 18 (3): 22–24.

————. 1980. Lessons about giftedness and creativity from a nation of 115 million overachievers. *Gifted Child Quarterly* 25:10–14.

Undheim, J. 1981. On intelligence IV: Toward a restoration of general intelligence. *Scandinavian Journal of Psychology* 22:251–65.

Ward, V. 1960. The role and nature of theory in the education of the gifted. *Educational Theory* 10 (3): 1–7.

————. 1975. Program organization and implementation. In *Psychology and education of the gifted,* eds. Barbe and Renzulli, 295–302. New York: Irvington.

————. 1975. Basic Concepts. In *Psychology and education of the gifted.* eds., Barbe and Renzulli, 61–71. New York: Irvington.

Weiner, B. 1980. The role of affect in rational (attributional) approaches to human motivation. *Educational Researcher* 9 (7): 4–11.

Wrightstone, J. 1960. Observational techniques. In *Encyclopedia of educational research,* ed. Harris, 927–33. New York: Macmillan.

Young, C. 1964. A survey of general systems theory. *General Systems* 9:61–80.

Zaffran, R., and N. Colangelo. 1977. Counseling the gifted and talented students. *Gifted Child Quarterly* 21 (3): 305–21.

PUBLICATIONS OF EDUCATIONAL ORGANIZATIONS, LEARNED SOCIETIES, AND GOVERNMENTAL AGENCIES

Aschner, M., and C. Bish, eds. 1965. *Productive thinking.* Washington: National Education Association.

Bereday, G., and J. Lauwerys, eds., 1961. *The Year Book of Education 1961: Concepts of excellence in education.* London: Evans Brothers.

————. 1962. *The Year Book of Education 1962: The gifted child.* London: Evans Brothers.

Cook, D. 1966. *Program evaluation and review technique, applications to education.* U.S. Department of Health, Education and Welfare, Office of Education, OE-12024, Monograph No. 17. Washington: United States Government Printing Office.

Department of Education and Science, HM I Series: Matters of Discussion 4. 1977. *Gifted children in middle and comprehensive secondary schools.* London: Her Majesty's Stationary Office.

BIBLIOGRAPHY

Elliot, R. 1971. Versions of creativity. In *Proceedings of the Philosophy of Education Society of Great Britain*, eds. Peters et al. 5 (2): 139–52.

Friedman, P. 1980. *Teaching the gifted and talented oral communication and leadership*. Washington: National Education Association.

Gavian, R., ed. 1958. *The social education of the academically talented* (Curriculum Series No. 10). Washington: National Council for the Social Studies, a department of the National Education Association.

Hindess, E. 1972. Forms of knowledge. In *Proceedings of the Philosophy of Education Society of Great Britain*, eds. Peters et al. 6 (2): 164–75.

Hollingworth, L. 1936. The development of personality in highly intelligent children. *Fifteenth Yearbook of the Department of Elementary School Principals*, 272–81. Washington: National Education Association.

Holmes, B. 1961. Polytechnical education in the U.S.S.R. *Bulletin (reprint) of the University of London Institute of Physics and the Physical Society*, 58–62.

Hoyle, E., and J. Wilks. 1976. *Gifted children and their education*. London: Her Majesty's Stationary Office.

Kaplan, S. 1975. *Providing programs for the gifted and talented: A handbook*. Reston, U.S.: Council for Exceptional Children.

Kershaw, J., and R. McKean. 1959. *Systems analysis and education*. Report to the Ford Foundation, RM-2473-EF. Santa Monica, CA: Rand Corporation.

Maker, J. 1975. *Training teachers for the gifted and talented. A comparison of models*. Reston, VA: Council for Exceptional Children.

Martinson, R. 1975. *The identification of the gifted and talented*. Reston, VA: Council for Exceptional Children.

Olton, R. et al. 1967. *The development of productive thinking skills in fifth grade children*. Washington: ERIC (document 021).

Paschal, E. 1960. *Encouraging the excellent: Special programs for the gifted*. New York: Fund for the Advancement of Education.

Phenix, P. 1977. Schema for an ethical analysis of affective dimensions in education. In *Feeling, valuing, and the art of growing: Insights into the affective*, eds. Berman and Roderick, 60–6. Washington: Association for Supervision and Curriculum Development.

Pierce, J. 1962. The bright achiever and under-achiever: A comparison. In *The yearbook of education 1962: The gifted child*, eds. Bereday and Lauwreys, 143–54. London: Evans Brothers.

Quinton, A. 1971. Authority and autonomy in knowledge. In *Proceedings of the philosophy of Education Society of Great Britain*, eds. Peters et al. 5 (2): 201–15.

Renzulli, J. 1975. *A guidebook for evaluating programs for the gifted and talented* (a working draft). Ventura, CA: Office of the Superintendent of Schools.

Runions, R. 1982. *Stewardship: Training the gifted as community mentors* (Contract No. 400-81-0031). Washington: National Institute of Education.

Sisk, D. 1976. *Teaching gifted children*. Project developed in conjunction with a federal grant from Title V, Section 505. Washington: United States Government Printing Office.

———. 1978. What is leadership training for the gifted? In *Proceedings of the Third Annual Northern Virginia Conference of Gifted/Talented Education*, ed. Orloff, 24–30.

Wall, G. 1974. Moral autonomy and the liberal theory of moral education. In *Proceedings of the philosophy of education Society of Great Britain*, eds. Peter et al. 8 (2): 222–36.

Ward, V. et al. 1962. *The gifted student: A manual for program improvement*. Atlanta: Southern Regional Education Board.

Ward, V., and H. Jellen. 1979. Personality structure and curricular differentiation: A synthesis in gifted education. In *Proceedings of the Fourth Annual Northern Virginia Conference on Gifted/Talented Education*, ed. Orloff, 42–52.

White, J. 1974. Intelligence and the logic of the nature-nurture issue. In *Proceedings of the Philosophy of Education Society of Great Britain*, eds. Peters et al. 3 (1): 30–51.

Wilson, P. 1974. Interests and educational values. In *Proceedings of the philosophy of Education Society of Great Britain*, eds. Peters et al. 8 (2): 181–99.

UNPUBLISHED MATERIALS

Jellen, H. 1981. A multi-lingual glossary for differential education for the gifted (DEG). Ph.D. thesis, University of Virginia.

Renzulli, J., and V. Ward. 1969. Diagnostic and evaluative scales for differential education for the gifted (DESDEG). Storrs and Charlottesville: University of Connecticut and University of Virginia.

Rip, A. 1980. Science and society education in Dutch schools. Paper presented at the University of London Institute of Education, London, UK.

Rumelhart, D., and P. Norman. (in press). Accretion, tuning and restructuring: Three modes of learning. In *Semantic factors in cognition*, eds. Klatsk and Cotton. Hillsdale, U.S.: Erlbaum Associates.

Shuter, R. 1964. An investigation of hereditary and environmental factors in musical ability. Ph.D. thesis, University of London.

HANS G. JELLEN completed his doctoral studies at the University of London and the University of Virginia in 1981, receiving a Ph.D. in the Psycho-social Foundations of Education. Between 1974 and 1978, he worked as a teacher of the gifted and talented in the Virginia Beach Public School System. He has coauthored two texts on leadership training of teachers and students as well as student interest and motivation. He also has published on differential education of the gifted in numerous articles in international journals. His Fulbright Award (1984–85) allowed him to work on policy, programming, and testing for the gifted in the Federal Republic of Germany.

JOHN R. VERDUIN, Jr., holds a Ph.D. in Curriculum with a Sociology cognate from Michigan State University. He spent five and a half years in public school teaching in the area of science and mathematics and has been a university professor and administrator for 24 years. His six years in administration involved work in undergraduate education, teacher education and student teaching. He is the author or coauthor of eight books and many articles in curriculum, instruction and teacher education. Dr. Verduin was on the State Advisory Council for the State of Illinois Gifted Program for seven years, chairing the council in 1984/85.